Sculpturing TOTEM POLES

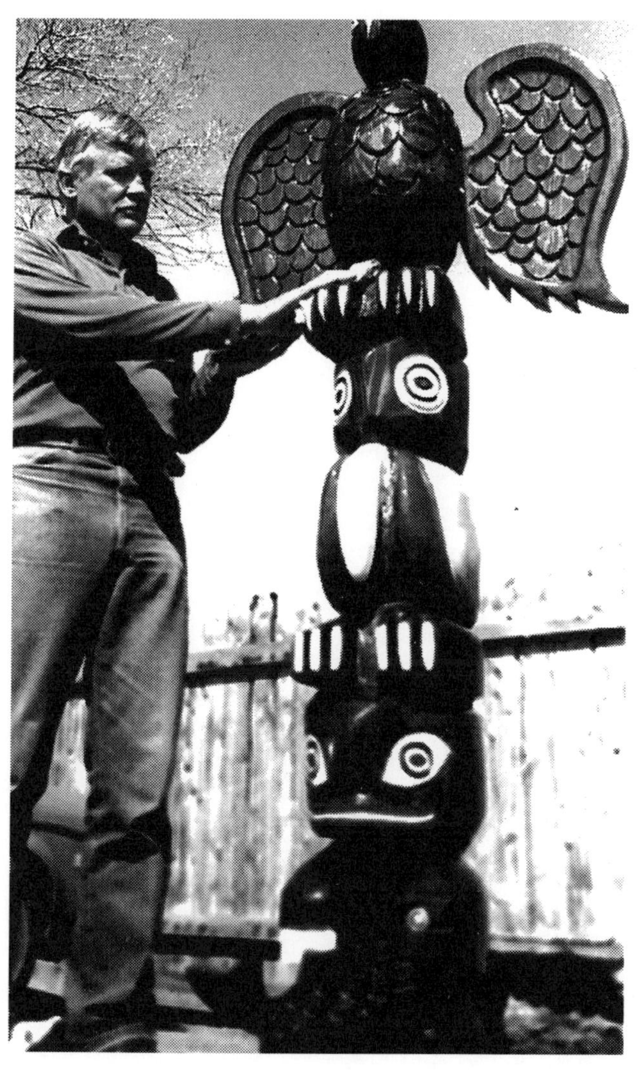

By Walt Way

Artwork by Walt Way
Edited and prepared by Jack Ekstrom
Copyright © 1985, 1995 by Walt Way

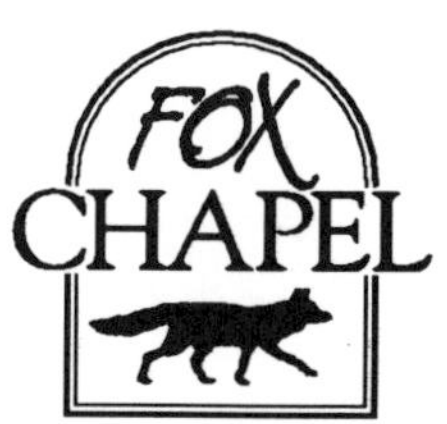

PO Box 7954
Lancaster, PA 17604-7954

TABLE OF CONTENTS

Library of Congress Cataloging in Publication Data

Way, Walt 1929

Sculpturing Totem Poles.

Bibliography: p.

Includes index.

1. Wood-carving- Northwest coast of North America. 2. Sculpture- Northwest coast of North America. 3. Totem poles- Northwest coast of North America. 4. Indians of North America- Northwest coast of North America- Sculpture. 5. Indians of North America- Northwest coast of North America- Wood-carving 1. Title.

TT199.7W39 1985 731.4'62 85-666

ISBN 1-56523-061-2

I
Origin and Significance of **TOTEM POLES**

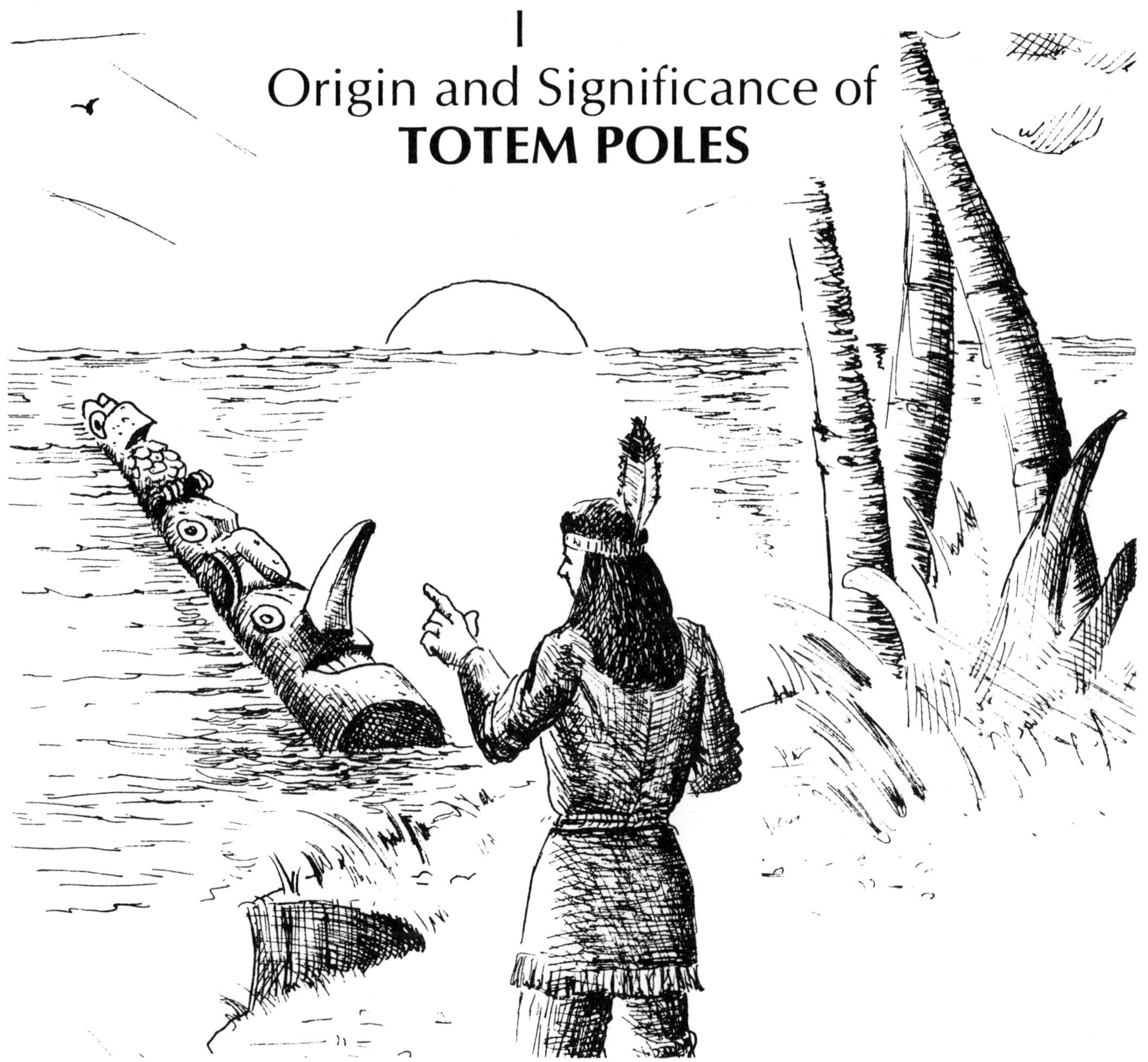

THE SOURCE

The creation of totem poles by the Indians of what is now the northwest United States, British Columbia, and Alaska was begun many, many years ago. Historians and anthropologists disagree on when and how the art got its start in North America. Wilson Duff has established that totem poles were a part of the culture of the peoples of the northwest coast in the late 18th century before Europeans came to the region. The most prolific era of carving (probably due to the availability of more efficient metal tools) was from around 1840 to 1880.

One theory has it that these Indians first discovered the art indirectly from earlier cultures in the South Sea Islands. Discarded Polynesian totems could have been carried by wind and sea to North America's shores where Kwakiutl, Haida, and other coastal Indian tribes observed the fascinating characters carved on the logs and decided to create local renditions for their own uses. Anyway, this is a good hypothesis.

WHY COASTAL INDIANS?

This theory of discarded sea-carried poles explains one of several probable reasons that only coastal Indian tribes have carved the large totems we still admire. Another is that the giant cedar trees were available as raw material for several uses; shelter, utensils, and for this magnificent art form, the totem pole. Perhaps more important, many of the coastal tribes stayed put, unlike the more nomadic tribes in North America, because food in the forms of fresh seafood, ducks, elk, deer, and bear were all around them. The Indians were able to gather food in the summer and use reserves for drying and preserving so that winter would not be a time of want.

With food, shelter, and relative stability in a reasonably moderate climate, artist-carvers could be supported by the chiefs of the tribes and were given time to do their beautiful work. We modern carvers should be so lucky!

THE SIGNIFICANCE OF TOTEMS

Totem poles were used to decorate doorways of houses, the framework of houses, or were free-standing poles. The latter are most commonly known and admired by people today. Although there were several classes of free-standing totems, the ones probably most often pictured and well-known in our day are the memorial, potlatch, and heraldic totem poles.

The memorial totem had phratries (i.e. figures of characters) up and down the length of the pole depicting the memorable and admired deeds of a great chief or hunter.

The potlatch pole was a center of attraction for a celebration by a chief after a great battle, hunt, or fishing exp

lac" of the times for a wealthy chief. It also appears that most significant poles were given credibility through having a potlatch ceremony where guests were invited, gifts given, and the totem's story told.

Heraldic poles were carved using the phratry of a husband and wife and telling their tribal history. The man's phratry was at the top; the woman's at the bottom. Rank or status was thus given to males with a superior position in totem sculpture. Even today we speak in metaphor of people or objects being rated as "high" or "low" on the totem pole of life's value systems.

Once carved and painted, the poles were left to withstand the ravages of time and weather without repair lest the spirits of ancestors be disturbed in the process of renovation.

If the reader is interested in learning more about the origin and significance of totem poles, a bibliography is included at the end of this book.

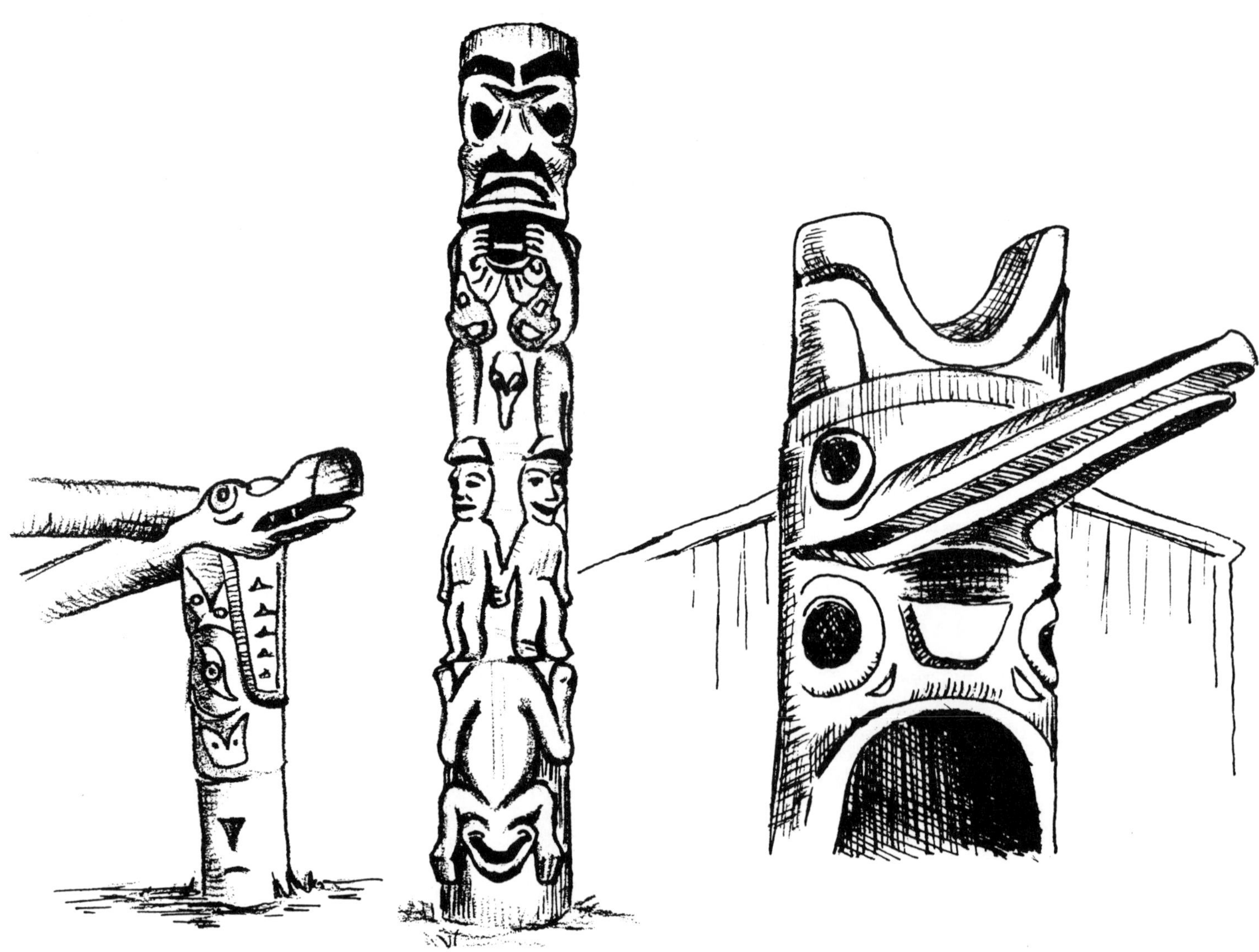

House posts. **Free standing.** **Doorway.**

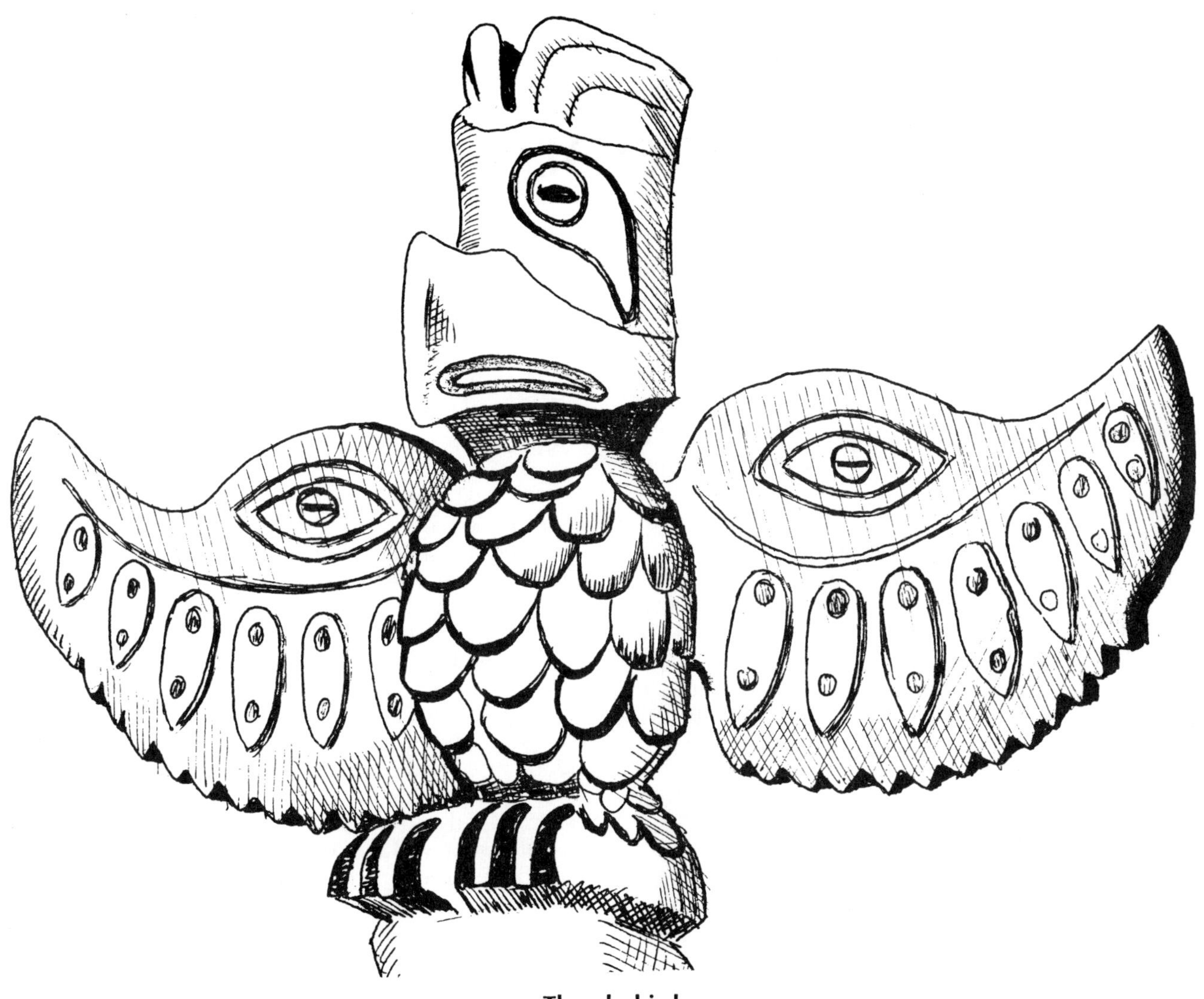

Thunderbird.

ANIMALS OR GHOULISH CHARACTERS CHOSEN AS PHRATRIES

The Indians felt a closeness with animals and all realms of existence—the water, earth, sky, and the land of the dead. Some of the characters used for totems symbolize this belief in a "oneness" of humans, animals, and spirits with nature.

The thunderbird was the fictitious protector of the Kwakiutl Indians. Its huge beak, piercing eyes, sharp claws, and magnificent wingspread combined artfully to strike fear into an approaching enemy and make him reluctant to attack a village with such an imposing protector. This phratry is my favorite to carve.

The Haida eagle was another beauty. Its high altitude flights and exceptional vision were said to forewarn the chief of an approaching enemy so the tribes could be prepared for danger.

The bear's strength served to protect a tribe as the bear would become transformed into a warrior and destroy an entire enemy tribe. With the addition of a salmon in its paws, it would ensure good fishing for the tribe.

The frog carved in a climbing or descending posture on the pole had a renowned aquatic sense to warn the tribe about the perils of deep water.

The raven was known for its wisdom. This long-beaked bird with folded wings would advise a chief as to the best times for hunting or fishing and even when to attack an enemy tribe.

These and other symbols of importance in the lives of the early Indians, when carved on logs, created an art form of simple eloquence and mystique which is still admired and sought by collectors today. Only the shaman, the tribe's storyteller, or the carver who was given some freedom of artistic expression, could explain some of the phratries such as the rather ghoulish faces we see on poles in museums or "live" phratries on poles still standing in the northwest regions.

A modern-day beginning carver would do well to "borrow" these phratries while gaining confidence and experience in the art. New and original phratries will come with experience and imagination. You may even want to tell your story on a totem pole one day.

II
About
WOODS

PLAN AHEAD

If you choose to carve from a raw timber, as I do, you should plan ahead far enough to see that you have one or more seasoned logs available of the size you require. Paul Luvera, an Italian immigrant to Ancortes, Washington in the early 1900's, has carved many beautiful totems using native Washington cedar which had been squared-off to perhaps 10" by 10" or 14" by 14" width. Whatever width and length of log he required, he purchased from a nearby sawmill.

Residents of other states may have trouble, as I did, finding milled and cured poles of this kind. An obvious advantage of the "squared" pole is that patterns of the phratries can be laid out a little more easily and drawn on the flat surfaces of a squared log than on naturally round peeled logs.

Ponderosa or Engleman pine and fir logs can be cut in the Rocky Mountain regions with permission from the Forest Service or purchased from a sawmill. These are my favorites in Colorado. Spruce trees should be avoided as they invariably dry with spiraling cracks running the length of the log. Cottonwood, hackberry, oak, hickory, maple, sycamore, or other trees are native to many states and, although harder woods, they could be used for totems if straight enough and if they have few branches. Branches create hard-to-carve knots on the pole.

DRYING AND PREPARING YOUR LOG

Well, you might have been able to obtain a log that has been slowly seasoned at a sawmill and ready for carving. If so, you may want to skip to the next chapter.

If you cut a green tree, it would be best to let it dry while stored off the ground on blocks for about a year. I let them dry with the bark on and the cut-ends sealed with two coats of sealer. You can use Watco Water Seal or another brand of wood sealer for exposed surfaces.

For bark removal, a draw knife is the best tool to use. The procedure for this will be briefly described in the chapter on "Tools to Use". After the log is cleaned of its bark you may want to apply some more sealer to prevent further checking. No matter what you do, you will probably experience some "checking" or vertical cracks in your large log. You have several choices as to what to do. You can leave small cracks and assume that they are part of the "nature of the beasts" or you can fill the cracks. Some carvers use small wedges of the same wood fitted and glued into straight cracks. I use the auto mechanic's body filler, Cuz, which dries quickly and can be filed and sanded easily. This material takes stain or oil paint without being very noticeable if sanded smoothly. Rock Hard Putty does not work for me as it crumbles and falls out of the crevices.

Your log should now be ready for you to draw on your patterns and, finally, begin carving. Take your time; stand back and admire your progress at various stages. Time and a critical eye can help you avoid costly mistakes.

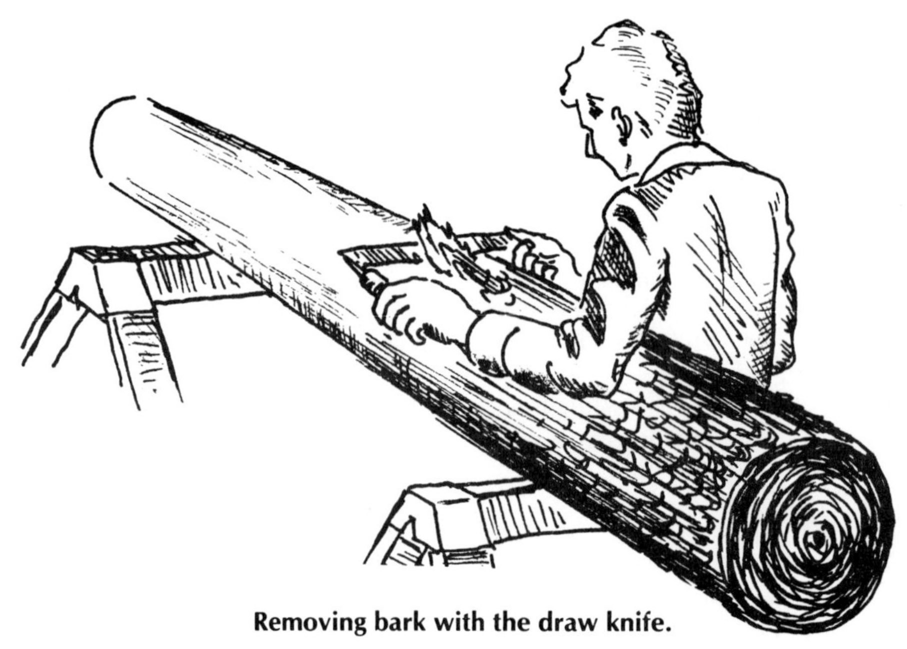

Removing bark with the draw knife.

III
TOOLS and EQUIPMENT

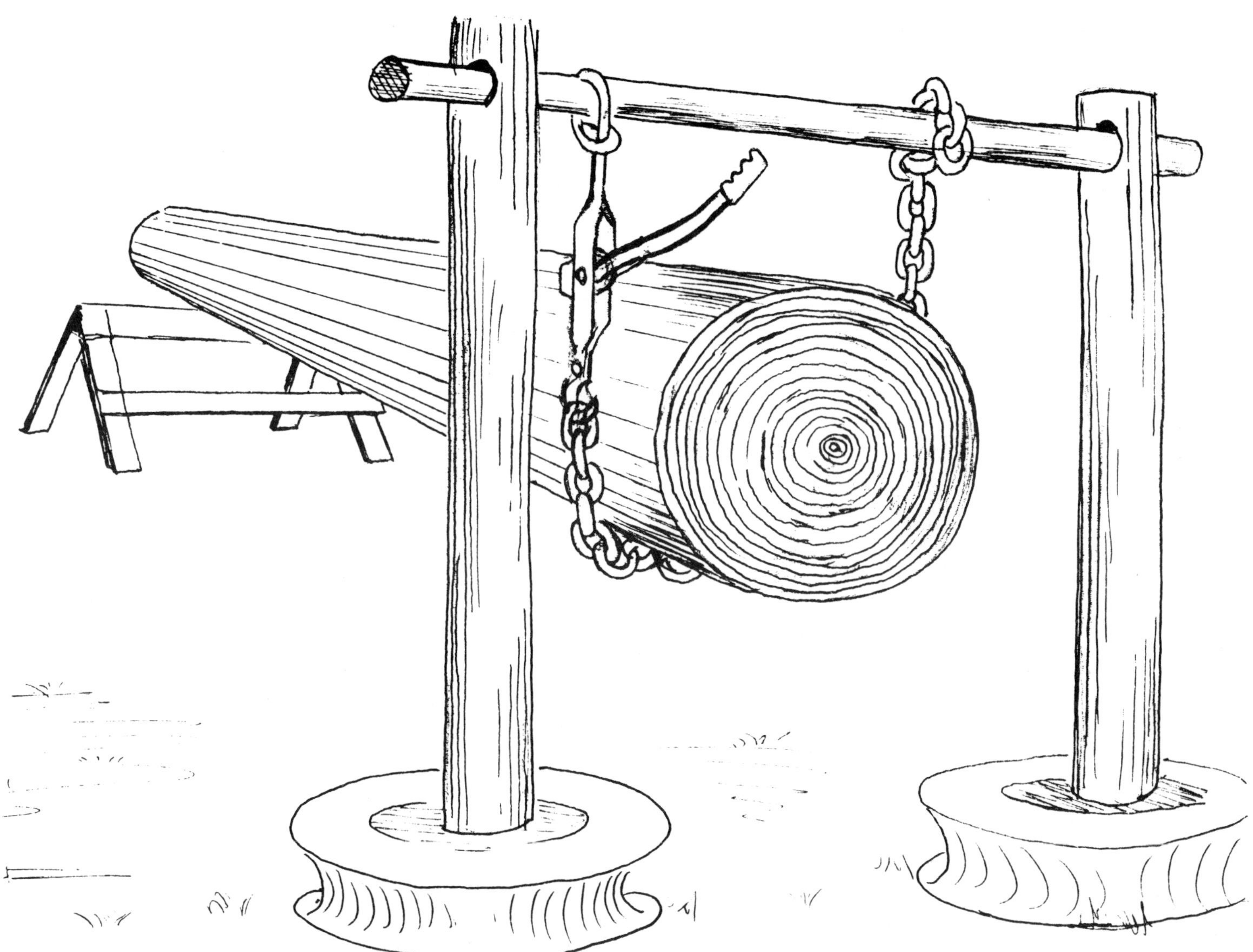

The "come along boomer".

LOG HOLDERS AND "TURNERS"

Unless you are a tree climber or a gymnast, you will want to carve your four-foot to thirty-foot totem with the pole in a horizontal position. The log can be set upon two sturdy sawhorses about 30" in height or you can use the surfaces of some old benches, short logs, or tables. Small pieces of wood tacked to the tops of the sawhorses and butted against the round log will help to keep your totem-in-the-round from slipping to either side.

For very long and heavy logs I use a sawhorse at one end and a special frame at the other end to support the log. I can turn the log from side to side with a come-along-boomer. This tool gives a mechanical advantage for easy turning so the carver can turn the totem or statue and have a better view while carving or painting. A local welder or mechanic may help you construct one.

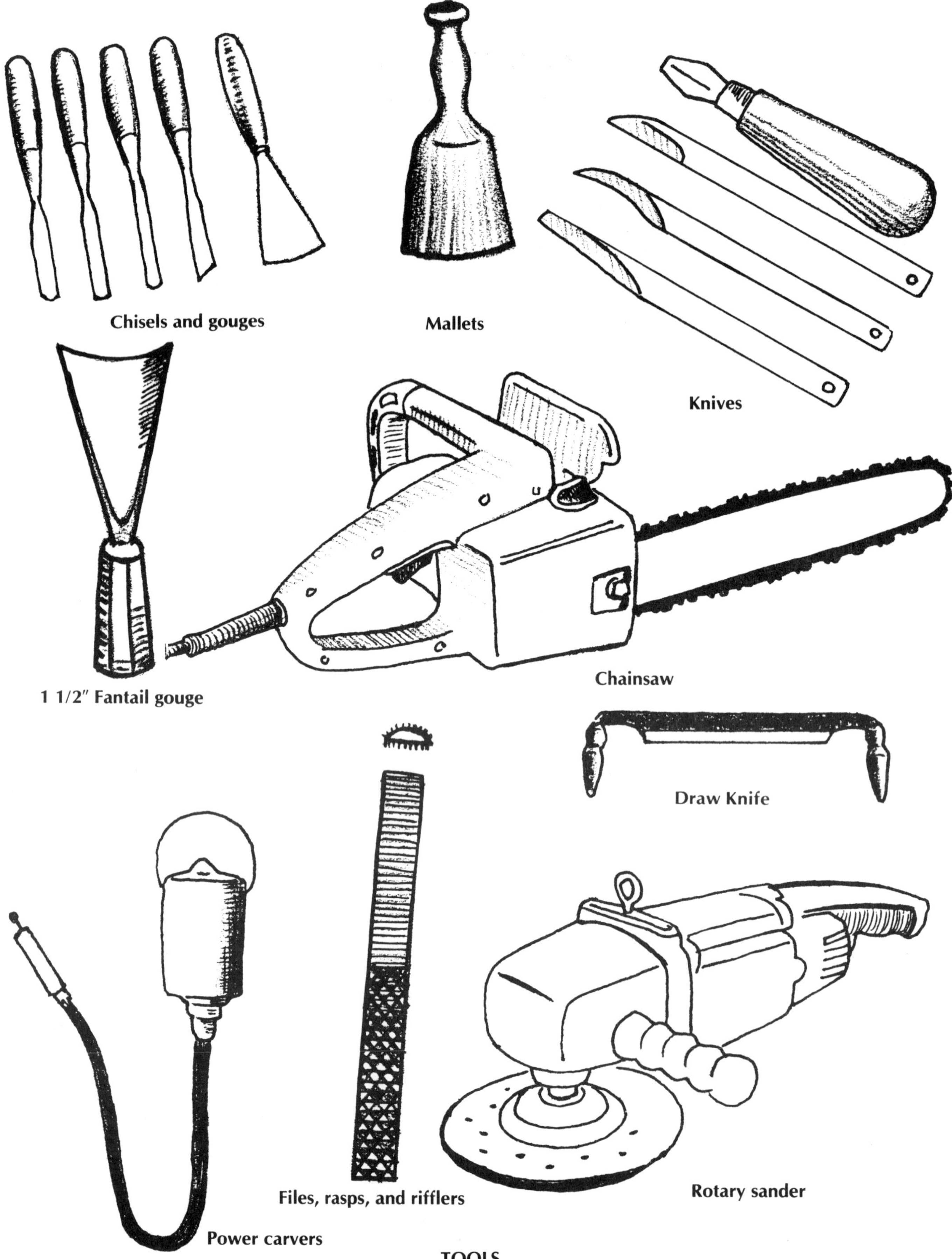
Chisels and gouges
Mallets
Knives
1 1/2″ Fantail gouge
Chainsaw
Draw Knife
Files, rasps, and rifflers
Rotary sander
Power carvers

TOOLS

ABOUT COLLECTING AND USING TOOLS

You don't need to own a lot of expensive tools to carve a large totem. My first totem was laboriously carved using a hatchet and sheath knife. Power tools for certain jobs will save you hours of time, but be prepared for the traditionalists who will say, "But the Indians didn't use power tools." Be assured that Indians would have used them just like the automobile and jet for transportation had they been available.

As you accumulate tools, I urge you to buy good ones. They will be safer and easier to use, keep a sharp edge longer, and, with proper care, last you a lifetime. Let's talk about tools in the order in which you are likely to use them.

THE TOOLS

A draw knife is useful for removing bark from the tree. You simply grasp both handles and "draw" the knife blade toward you, removing chunks of bark in the process. Loose bark can be removed with the hands or small tools usable for prying the bark away.

A chain saw is a must for removing large chunks of wood from the log and enabling you to get down close to the pattern. I removed literally hundreds of pounds of wood from a log four feet in diameter to "find" the outline of a coal miner I wanted to carve.

It was Michelangelo, the great Renaissance artist, who said that "in every piece of marble there is a statue. It is my task to find it." That profound statement has been useful to me—to keep in mind as I carve in wood. I stand back and look at the work frequently to see where I am with what I want the finished product to look like.

To use an electric chain saw you must be reasonably near an electric outlet. I use a Stihl E-10 electric chain with automatic chain oiling and a twelve inch bar. The saw weighs less than nine pounds and is not as tiring to use as my heavier, gas-powered Jonserud chain saw. A 100′ heavy duty extension cord gives me room to maneuver the length of a 30′ totem. As you gain experience with a chain saw you can use it as a "carving tool" to exacting dimensions of cutting and shaping. Never "force" a chain saw or power tool. Simply guide your power tool into the work.

Some wood sculptors use only a chain saw and leave the finished project with a rugged, rough-cut appearance. My preference, again, is to use this tool chiefly to remove large chunks of wood and to do some shaping and rounding-off.

Chain saws can be dangerous. The manufacturer's safety precautions should be carefully followed and it's not a good idea to use one without frequent rest periods.

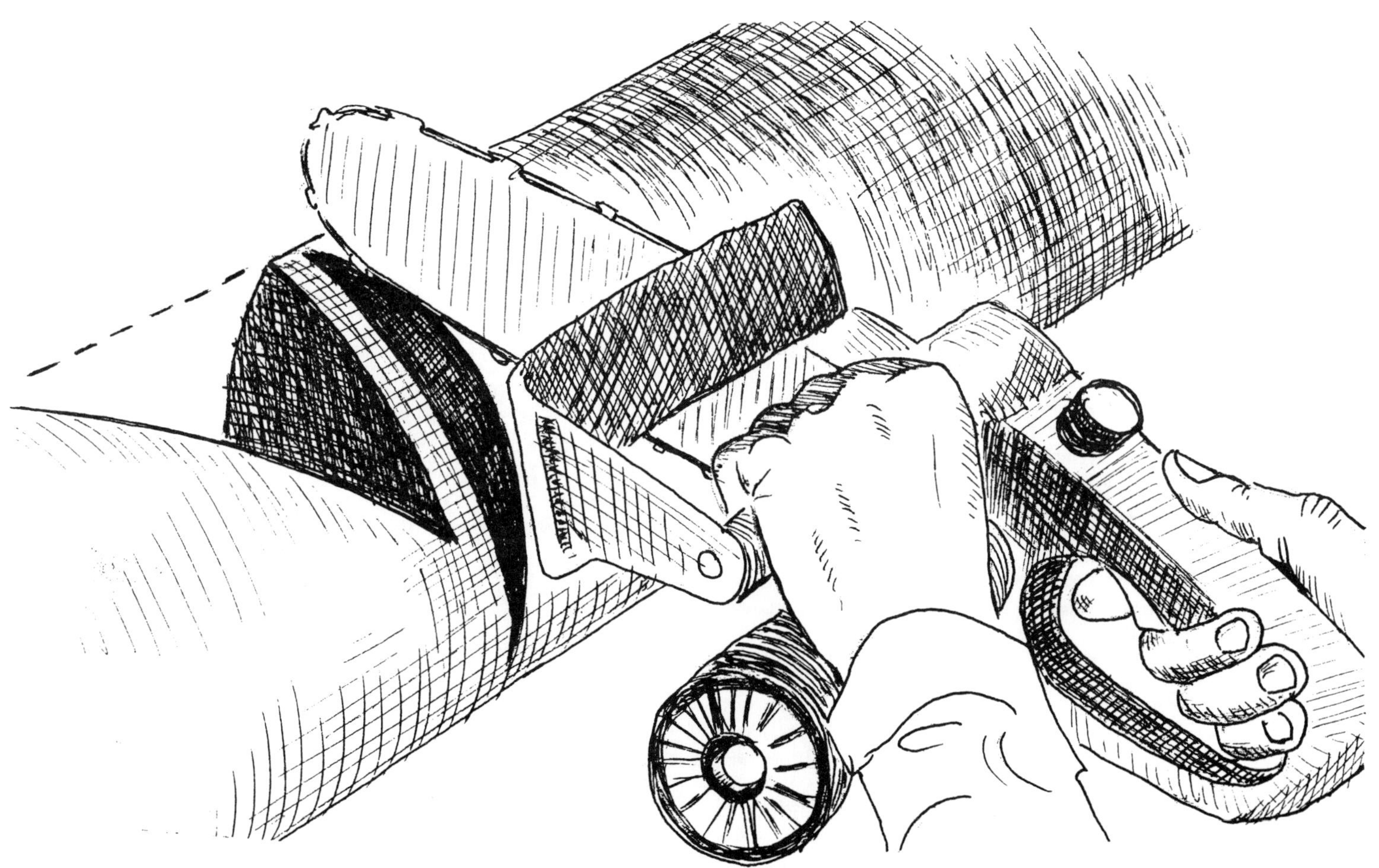

Chain saw cutting out a Thunderbird beak.

This time taken between cuts can also give you a chance to stand back and observe how you are progressing, as I have said before.

You may want to rent, or borrow, a chain saw for your first adventures with this tool, as good ones can cost from $185 to $400 by the time you get all the extras such as oil, tools, extension cord, carrying case, extra chain, and the like. The illustrations will help, but practice and experience will be your best "teacher" with a chain saw.

Gouges and mallets are useful for finer carving. I seldom use flat chisels as most of the work is rounded and gouges can be used more effectively to shape around mouths, beaks, eyes, and ears. One can either guide the gouge using both hands for delicate wood removal or tap the handle with a mallet when cutting away larger amounts of wood. Some carvers leave the gouge marks for effective texture and others prefer to sand the surfaces to a smooth finish. On my totems, I prefer to use a sanded finish.

A 1-1/2" fantail gouge is helpful for shaping large areas such as the head of the bear, the beak of the thunderbird, or the outline of the frog.

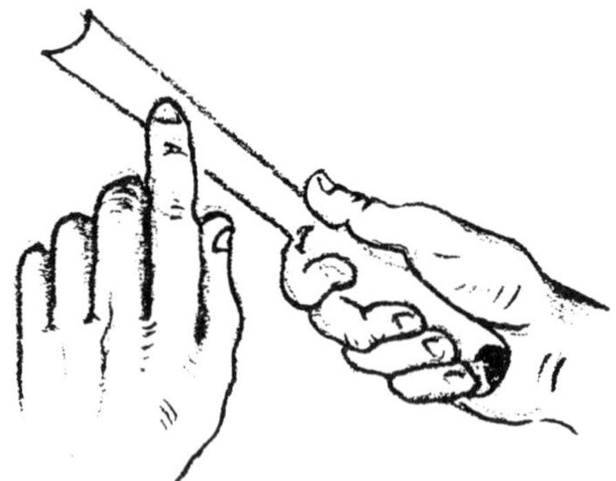

Using the gouge.

A 1/2" gouge provides more control in achieving yet finer cuts around such areas as eyes, mouths, thunderbird feathers, and bear feet. A 1/4" gouge can then bring you closer to the final shapes in exacting curved places around the features mentioned above and in the grooves of the winged phratries. A V-shaped parting tool can also help remove wood between the teeth of the beaver, to shape the space between claws, and the like.

Carving knives come in all shapes and sizes. You may already have a suitable pocket knife. The Warren tool with its various blades is a good tool for the final shaping of mouths, teeth, and eyes of the phratries. A knife blade is essential for detail and "finishing" work.

Wood files and rifflers are used to smooth and even shape the delicate areas around the facial features described above which are left rough and irregular after using gouges or knives. I use a common rasp rounded on one side and flat on the other. Half of each side is for rough work and half for medium filing. A curved riffler can put the final touches to spaces between teeth and around the eyes.

The six or seven inch rotary sander is an indispensible tool for my work. I have both. With coarse discs of sandpaper, the sander can quickly smooth and contour areas the length of the totem. A follow-up with medium or fine grade sandpaper discs saves hours of labor by hand, using sheets of sandpaper. These sanders are often on sale at stores like Sears or Wards and the sandpaper discs are also readily available. This is probably my most valuable tool—next to the chain saw.

The Foredom CC-30 hang-up model tool with flexible shaft and No. 44A handpiece is another time saver. It is a more heavy-duty tool than the Dremel tool and is used to "erase" the wood around eyes and in the grooves of the wings. I use a 134 Dremel burr or Foredom's VE4 steel burr in my Foredom tool for these shapes. Using a knife or gouge in these grooved areas takes more time and is more apt to cause splintering or irregular grooves, but it can be done and probably gives more of a "hand-carved look to your work—which is okay.

Again, there is no substitute for practice and experimentation. Each carver develops preference for tools with experience and there is no one answer for everybody. The finished product done to your standards is what counts—no matter what kind of tools you used to achieve the desired result.

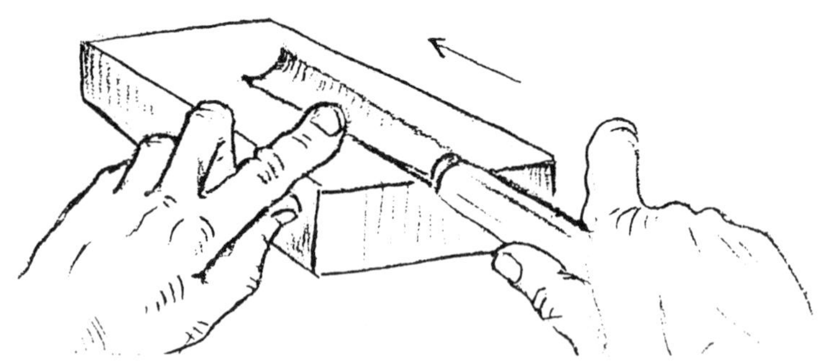

Sharpening the gouge.

SHARPENING TOOLS

There is nothing more tedious to a woodcarver than working with dull tools. With a little time and effort you can keep your tools in good shape. In most towns there are a few people who have the equipment for sharpening chains of chain saws and the teeth of hand saws. You can find them in the yellow pages.

Gouges and knife blades are relatively easy to sharpen. A cutlery storekeeper can demonstrate proper use of oil stones and leather strops. I use an Arkansas stone coated with mineral oil to keep an edge on knife blades and gouges. The cutting edge of a knife blade would always go toward the stone, starting close to you, and moving across the stone with a sliding motion from tip to handle. Tilt the dull edge of the blade about 15 degrees off the stone. Gouges are directed using both hands as shown, sharp edge forward and with a similar angle. Use a rotating motion, as the blade is rounded. With both knives and gouges, think of your action as being almost the same as if the stone were wood and you are "cutting into" the stone.

IV
The Four Foot **KWAKIUTL TOTEM**
"The Thunderbird Over A Bear—With Salmon"

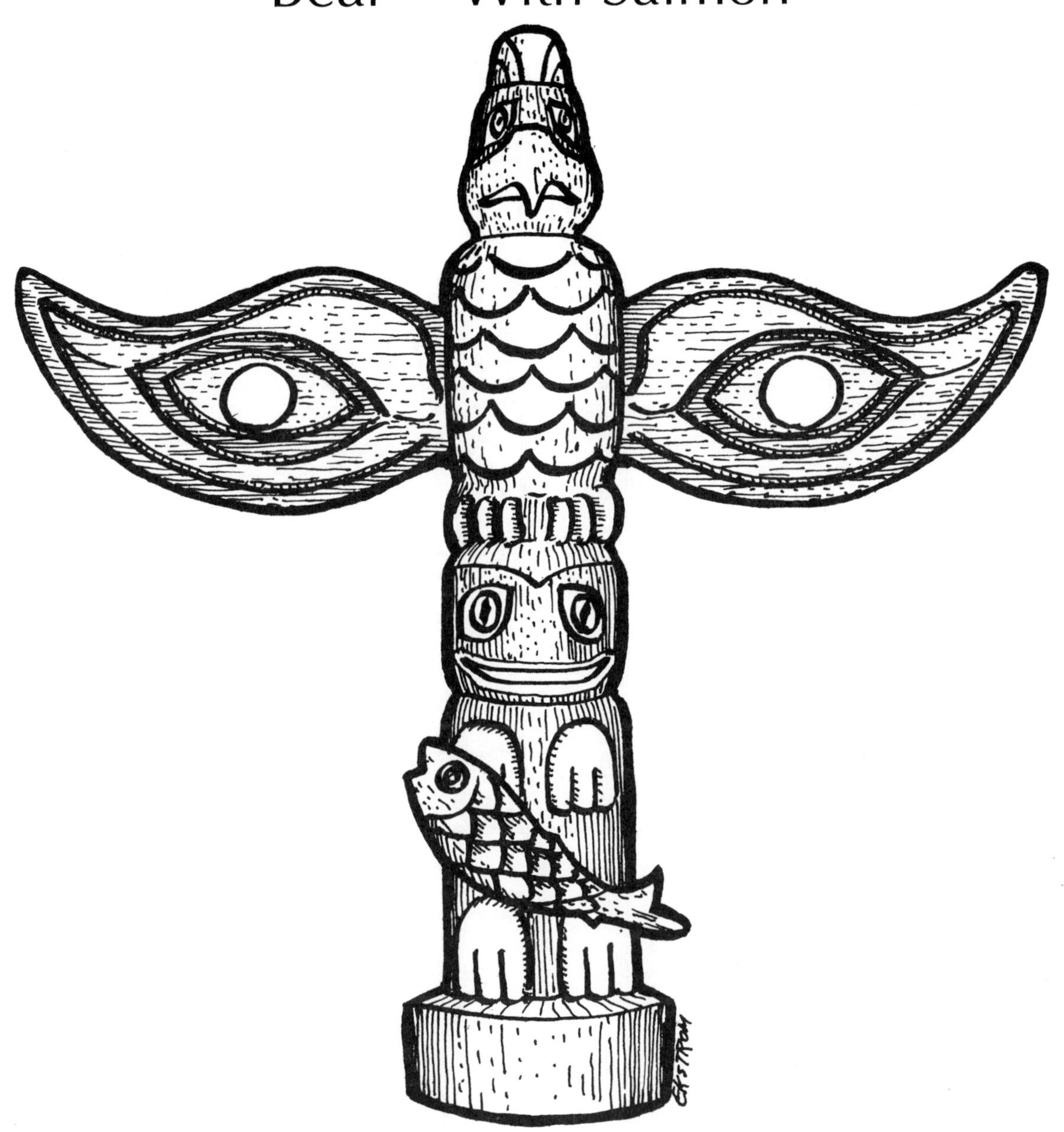

Now, for the fun of carving totem poles. We will describe in detail the procedure for carving two of my favorites. The first will be a four-foot Kwakiutl totem and the second will be a beautiful Haida Alaskan pole. The skills and experience you will gain from carving these two can then be applied to your next projects.

As I write this most important part, it is with some trepidation in rememberance of my own experiences with several "how to" books on carving. My editor suggests overdoing the narrative as it is frustrating to the reader to find that some directions which appear so important to one's progress are either missing or are glibly

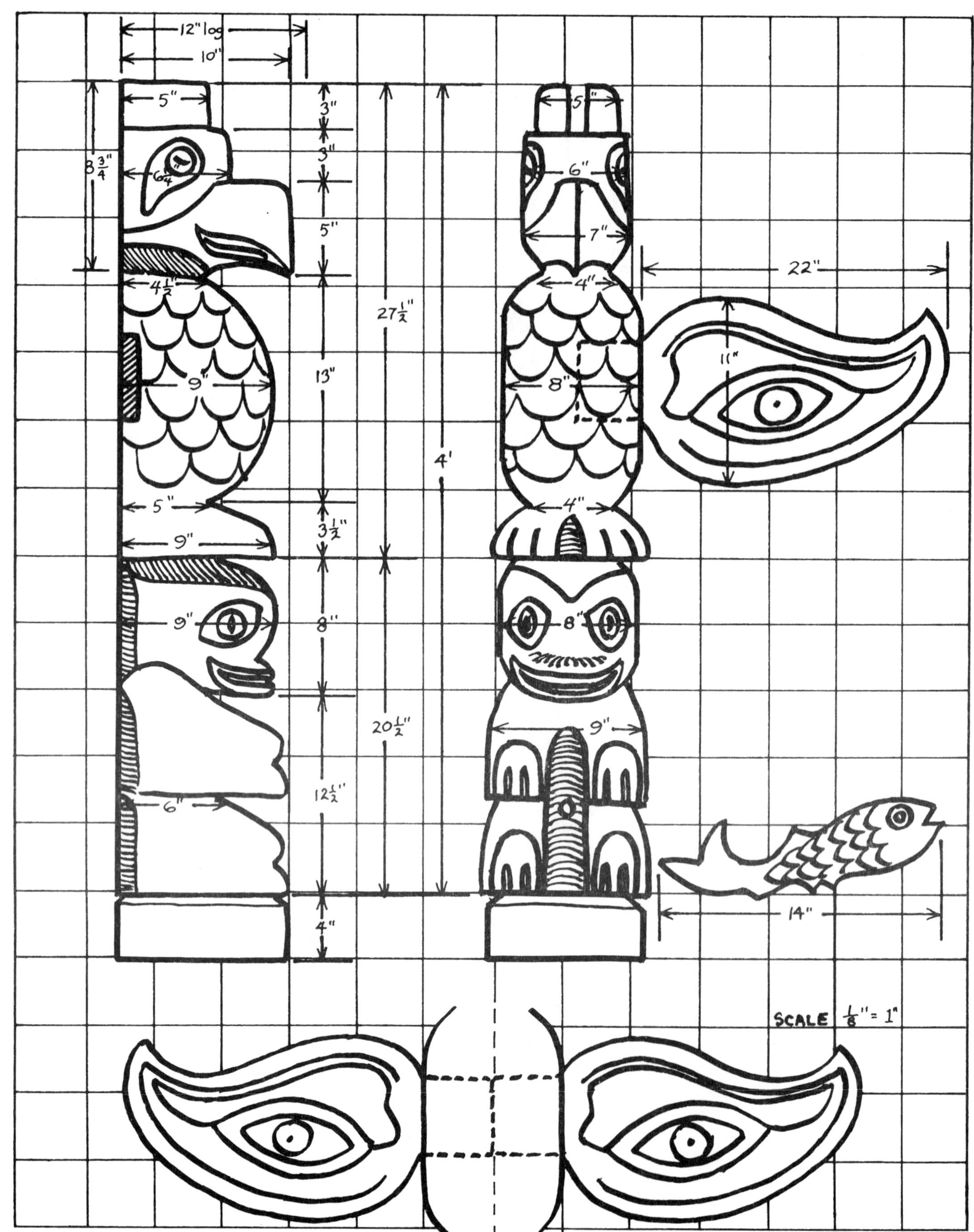

FOUR FOOT KWAKIUTL TOTEM

presented as though the beginner could "read between the lines" into the writer's mind.

With that said, it is also difficult for the writer-carver to foresee all the concerns of those who will attempt to convert the ideas, directions and patterns presented here into your own works of sculpture, I will do my best.

Before you lay tools to wood, recognize that you may make mistakes. In your first carvings, be cautious about cutting too deeply into your pattern. One can always cut off more wood but cannot easily rectify a problem of replacing wood you wanted to be there. A mark of a good carver, however, is to be able to cover up most minor mistakes by making minor alterations or repairs. Remember, every carving will be slightly different even if you use the same pattern.

Also, keep a record of your carving time in a small notebook. It's fun to "log" the hours and, believe me, the first question people will ask is, "How long did it take you to carve that?"

Totem poles (unlike statues) are made to be observed only from the front. The characters we will use are the same crests or phratries the Indians used back in the nineteenth century. They have a distinctive beauty all their own and are not supposed to look like real frogs, bears, or ravens.

The phratries should be centered up and down the pole with one phratry directly over the other so that you don't end up with the characters facing several different directions. Draw a line the length of the pole to designate center-front of your totem and then your phratries and their parts can be properly aligned. Feet and eyes are equally distant from the center line.

THE FOUR FOOT KWAKIUTL TOTEM

You can use any two phratries in a four foot totem pole. The thunderbird is effective with its spread wings for a lateral dimension and the bear with its salmon adds character to the front surface.

In carving this totem, I have used a ponderosa pine log four feet long and about twelve inches in diameter. A cedar log or squared 10" by 10" post would do. Whatever the wood, it should be reasonably soft and knot-free.

SET THE LOG

Lay the log horizontally on two saw horses about waist high, if possible. You can use blocks, benches, or old tables. Stabilize the log with wedges of wood so that it stays steady. The wood should have the bark removed and be sanded smoothly enough to draw on your pattern. Remember that the longer you let the raw timber dry before removing the bark up to a year the less chance for large checks or cracks in the log.

Again, you start by drawing the center line (top to bottom) for the front of your totem. This line should be kept on top facing the sky as you draw the pattern, make your cuts, and do most of the carving. We will refer often to this anatomical position of the log as it lies horizontally, the top or "above" being that side which faces up.

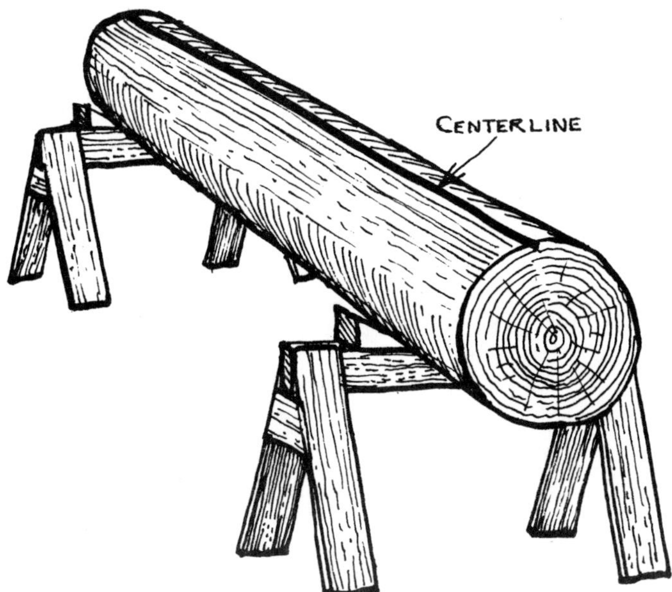

The peeled log with centerline.

SIDE VIEWS

Next, look at the side view pattern and use a Magic Marker or crayon to lay out the side views of your rough design on one side of the log; do the same thing on the other side of the log. Take your time as this is important. Starting at the top (and looking at the side view pattern) draw the side view dimensions of the thunderbird and bear on the log. If your log (or a square cut piece of wood) is not exactly 12" thick, this is no problem. Make the proportions as nearly the same as possible. To ensure a sense of proportion, just note that the cuts at the neck and feet of the thunderbird are deep into the log as are the cuts below the face of the bear and between the upper and lower legs. You will have to use judgement and a critical eye as to what looks right to you. Kneel some distance back from both sides of the log and take a look at your outline. Make changes, if

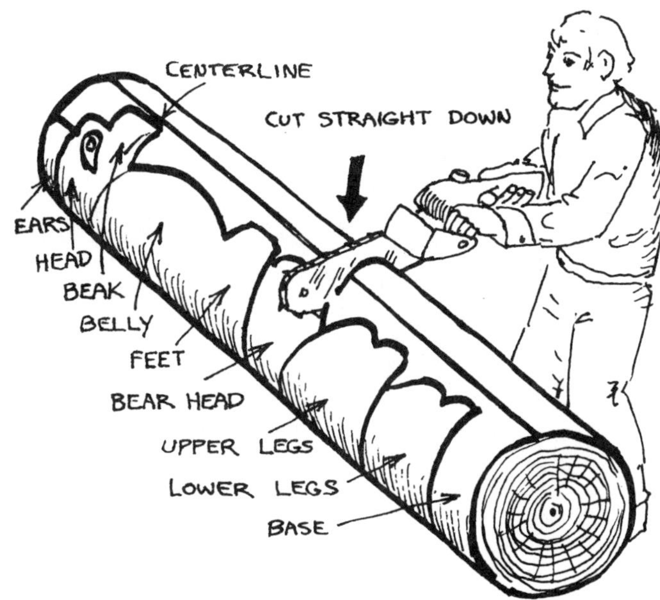

Make vertical cuts with the chainsaw.

needed, by sanding off markings you don't feel are right and correct them to your satisfaction.

LARGE CUTS

Now you are ready to use your chain saw (or hand saw if you wish) to make large cuts. Be careful, and watch for kickbacks of the chain saw if you jab the front end into the wood. Beginning with the thunderbird make vertical cuts down to your pattern from the top at the joints of ears and head, head and beak, beak and belly, and belly and feet. Make sure you don't cut too deeply on one side or the other. You may want to stop a half-inch or so from your pattern lines to be safe. Continue making vertical cuts at the joints of thunderbird feet and bear head, bear chin and upper legs, and between upper and lower legs.

Now let's remove the wood above the ears and head. Carefully make horizonatal cuts, starting again at the top of the thunderbird and removing the wood to 1/2" or so above the ears and the head.

To remove the excess wood over the beak, body and feet of the thunderbird and the head and legs of the bear, make cuts with the chain saw about 3/4" apart down close to your pattern lines. Again, be careful to go down the same amount on both sides. The thin shafts of wood can now be removed by using a fantail gouge or (with practice) using your chain saw held so that the blade cuts horizontally.

SMOOTHING

All of this cutting can be done with chisels and gouges, but it takes a lot of time just to remove excess wood so you can "find" the frontal outline of the phratries below. Now, with all the excess wood removed above the front surface outline, use a wood file and then a rotary sander with a coarse aluminum oxide sandpaper disc to smooth the top surfaces close to your pattern lines on either side. The curves on the thunderbird beak, the belly, feet, and bear detail can be done later. Look at the drawings often, and compare with your progress. At this stage you should have the front view squared off to approximate dimensions.

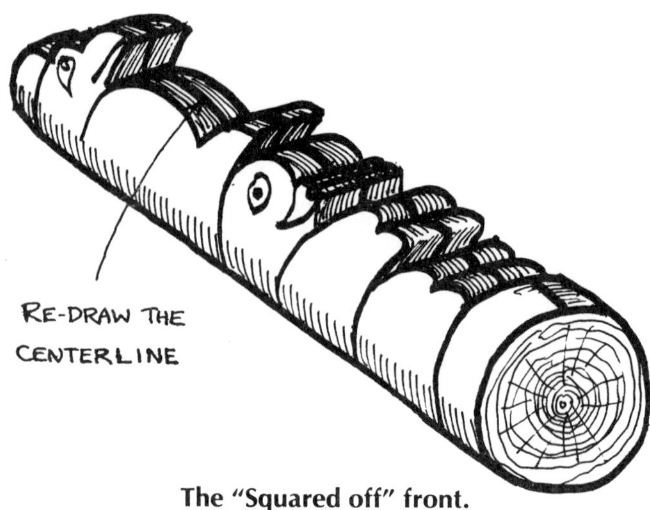

The "Squared off" front.

SEPARATE TOP EARS

Make the cut between the ears on top to separate them. The cut should be about an inch wide. By kneeling at the head end, you can quickly draw lines for the

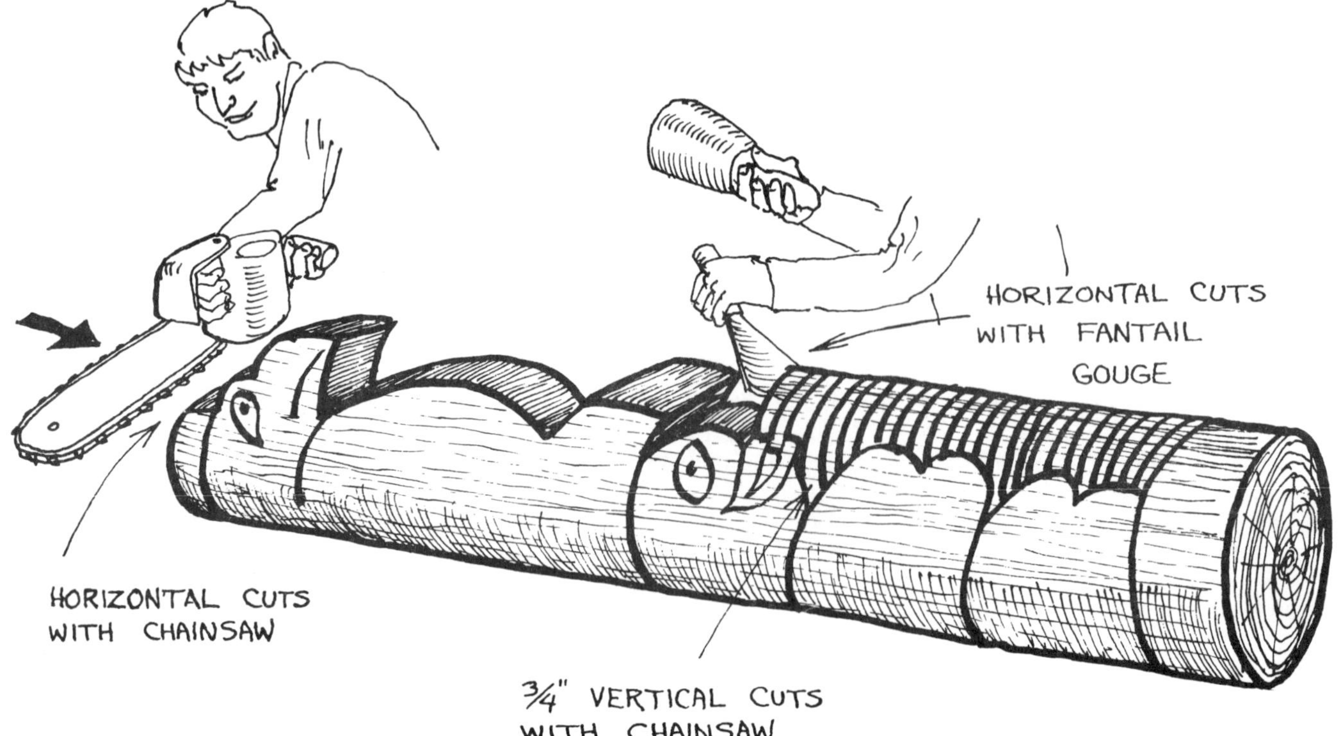

The horizontal cuts.

top view of the ears by extending front view lines for separation to the top of the ears and straight down the top. Make cuts with your chain saw at the inside edges of both ears and one in the center between them. Then remove the wood with a 1/2" gouge or further cuts with your chain saw.

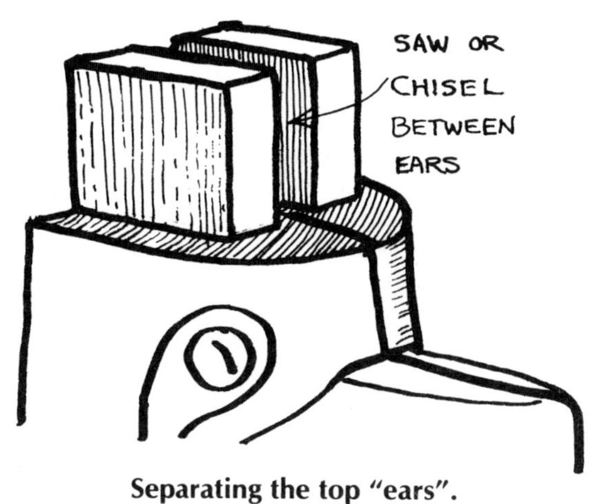

Separating the top "ears".

Since you have removed all the top surface wood except for the beak, you will have to redraw your center line down the length of your totem.

ROUNDING THE THUNDERBIRD HEAD

The next step is to give shape and "roundness" to the phratries. Notice first that the widest parts in the pattern of the front view are about 4" narrower than the side view. Let's start with the thunderbird beak.

6"
7"
FRONT VIEW

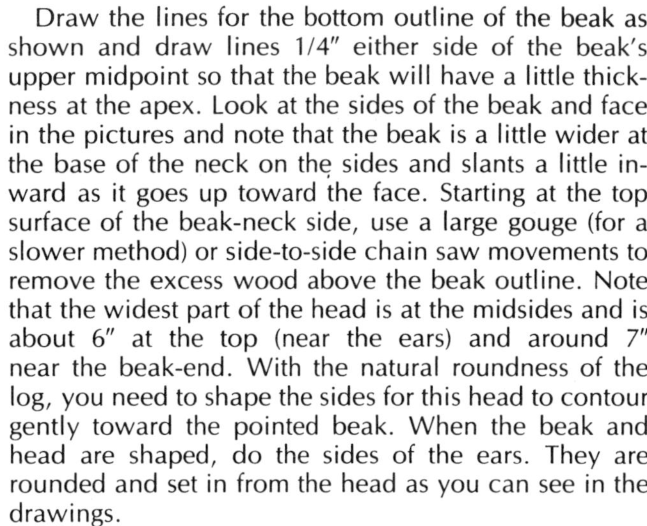

Draw the lines for the bottom outline of the beak as shown and draw lines 1/4" either side of the beak's upper midpoint so that the beak will have a little thickness at the apex. Look at the sides of the beak and face in the pictures and note that the beak is a little wider at the base of the neck on the sides and slants a little inward as it goes up toward the face. Starting at the top surface of the beak-neck side, use a large gouge (for a slower method) or side-to-side chain saw movements to remove the excess wood above the beak outline. Note that the widest part of the head is at the midsides and is about 6" at the top (near the ears) and around 7" near the beak-end. With the natural roundness of the log, you need to shape the sides for this head to contour gently toward the pointed beak. When the beak and head are shaped, do the sides of the ears. They are rounded and set in from the head as you can see in the drawings.

Cut enough wood (about 3/4") straight above the head contours on each side to form the ears. Now, smooth the head, beak, and ears using a rotary sander and wood files for hard to reach places.

ROUND THE BODY

The belly of the thunderbird is next. Starting from the top mid-line of the belly, begin to round off the square

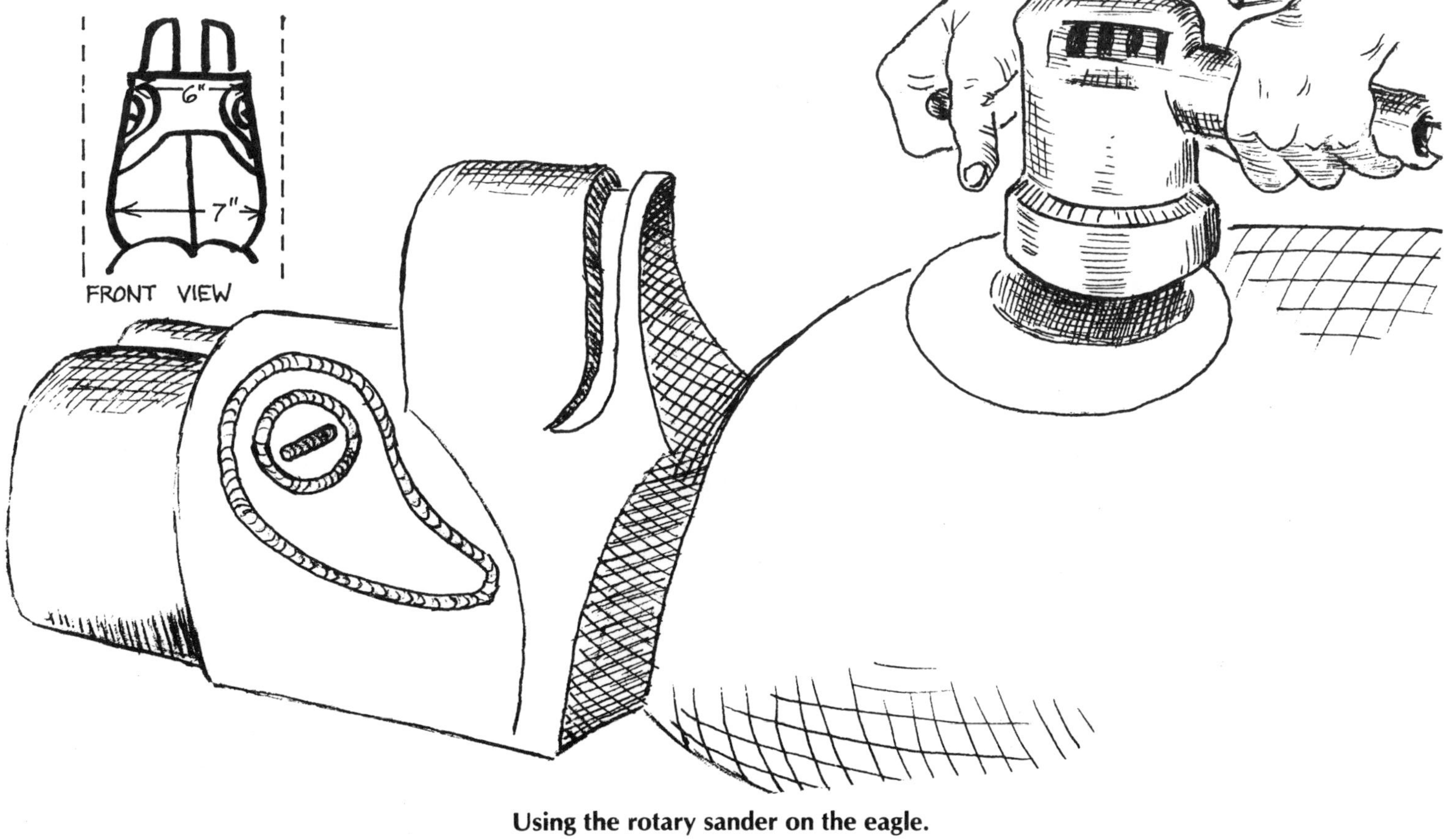

Using the rotary sander on the eagle.

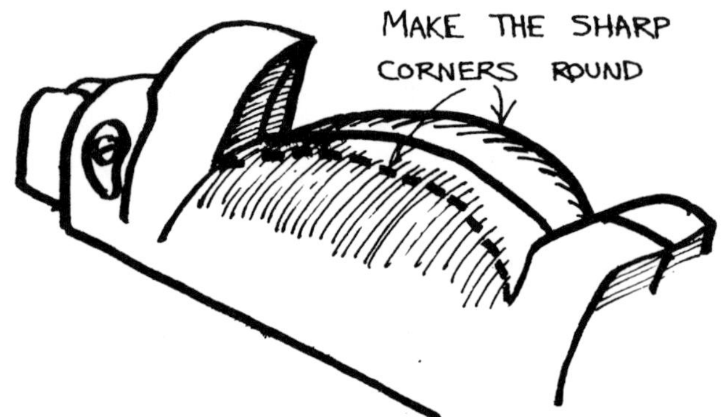

Rounding the thunderbird belly.

edge using a large gouge or chain saw. I use my electric chain saw with side-to-side easy motions and can shape the belly in a few minutes. Using each tool, be sure to check often and compare your work with the drawings to see that you are getting the belly rounded equally on both sides and sloping inward at the feet and neck. Your rotary sander is a good tool for final shaping and smoothing of the belly.

THE FEET

The feet of the thunderbird can be designed in several ways. You may wish to have three little toes as I have shown or make longer, pointed talons. The feet are a good project for your carving knife or 1/4″ gouge as you're now getting into the finer, smaller parts of the project. Simply draw on the wood the dimensions of the three toes (equally separated) and shape the feet, leaving 1-1/2″ or so between the feet. Slant the feet upward toward the body slightly from the front top of the toes and sides of the feet as shown in the diagram. Smooth these areas with wood files and sandpaper. Go back to the beak and shape the underside curves and angles, drawing lines first as shown in the pattern. Wait to draw in the eyes and mouth until the rest of the totem is carved to its basic design.

THE BEAR HEAD

Now use a method similar to that for the thunderbird to shape the bear head. Looking up from the base of the bear at where the bear chin will be, draw on the wood the shape of the bear's chin as shown on the drawing. The bear head is essentially straight up and down, and about 8″ at the widest part. Again, note that the widest parts are at the sides of the head with a slope toward the angular front of the face. Looking at the pictures and diagrams will give you your best guide as to how to proceed. As with the thunderbird beak, you can use either a chain saw or gouge to remove the wood above the lines and back to the top of the bear head. Note the slant of the bear head's top where it meets the feet of the thunderbird. Carve this with a 1/2″ gouge or carving knife. Use your rotary sander to smooth out the rough spots. Stand back and take a look. Is the shape about right? If not, shape it up some more.

Using a small (1/4″) gouge or carving knife, gently indent the area above the mouth. The deepest part is about 2″ above the chin at the front and only about an inch deep on top as it blends into the sloping portion of the face about three inches back to either side.

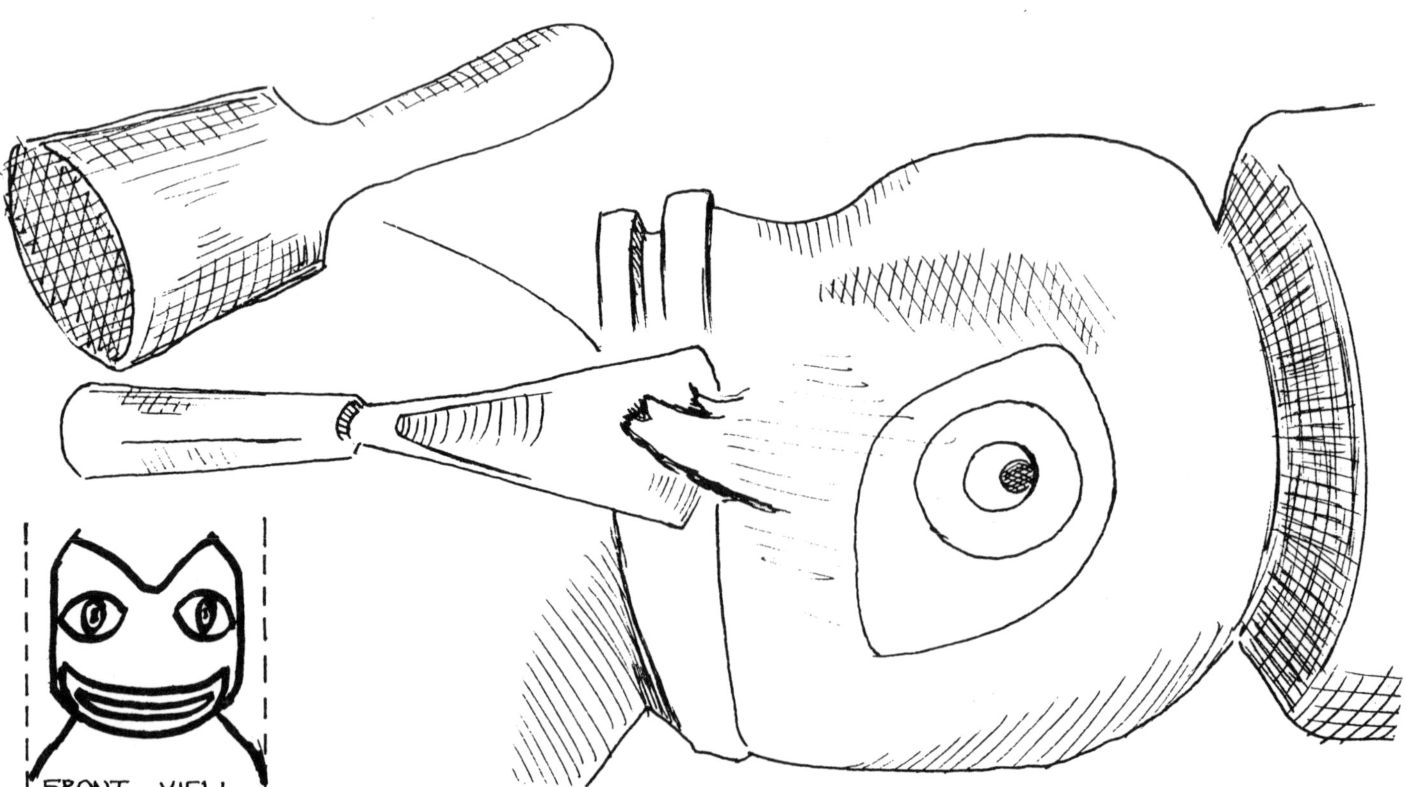

The broad shape of the bear head done with fantail gouge—for removal of large amounts of wood.

LEGS

In carving the legs of the bear, first separate them. Draw lines from the neck to the feet an inch to either side of the center line as shown. This two inch space (about neck deep) then needs to be carved out from the neck straight down to the base. You can use a chain saw or gouges for this work. Round off the inside edges of the legs with a wood file and medium coarse sandpaper. The entire top and sides of the totem should now be sanded and smoothed. Turn the totem over to sand the back of the log with your rotary sander, using coarse grit and then medium aluminum oxide discs.

Designs for the upper and lower toes of the bear can be drawn on now. Look at the pictures to place them correctly. Use a 1/4" gouge or carving knife to separate the toes going down to about 3/8".

THE FEATHERS

This is a "fun" task. Starting at the neck, draw the U-shaped feathers on the belly. Each "U" is about 1 1/4" wide and 1-1/2" from top to bottom, although it looks better if the feathers are slightly irregular. Note that the two feathers join at the center base of a U-shaped feather above. To give the appearance of depth to the feathers, carve out the space beneath the "U" of each feather about 1/2" and slope the feather gently toward the "U" below it. A little practice will give you "the hang of it".

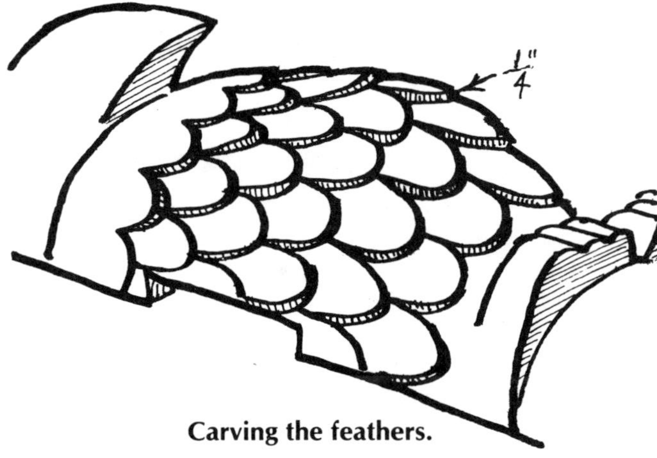

Carving the feathers.

EYES

Now, let's do the eyes and mouths of the two phratries. The eyes of the thunderbird are easier than they look. Use the template shown in scale of 1/8" to 1" actual size. Draw the template to correct size on a sheet of paper. Starting with the template of the right eye, I place it with a carbon underneath and draw on the wood with a pencil, changing it until it looks right. Carve out the grooves going to a depth of 1/4" or more using a carving knife or 1/4" gouge. If you have a high-speed Dremel or Foredom flexible shaft tool, you can save time by using a #134 Dremel burr and gently erasing the wood, moving the tip from right-to-left around the curves of the eye. Either way is fine, but take your time. Remember, the eyes "mirror the soul"—even of a totem pole.

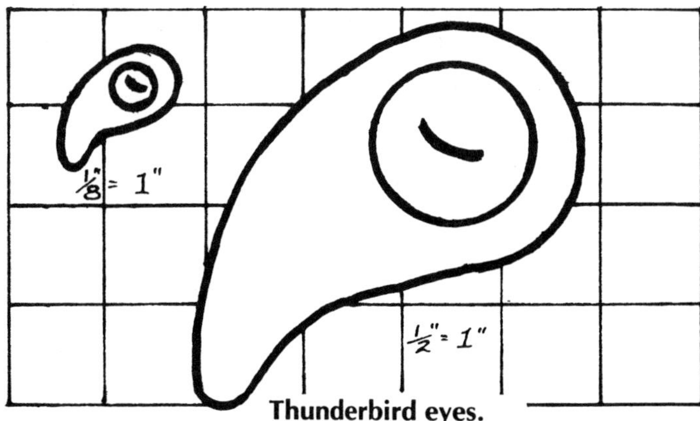

Thunderbird eyes.

When the eye is carved, use the "old paper carbon trick" to locate the other eye. Place an 8 1/2 x 11 sheet of paper (with one edge on the center line of the forehead and another at the top of the head) and blacken the area over the eye with a soft lead pencil. This will act as a "carbon paper". When you then turn the paper over, place the same edges against the center line and top of head, then trace the pattern on the left side. The eyes will thus be the same size and positioned accurately. You may have to darken your lines a little so you can have a good, clear pattern. Carve the left eye as you did the right one.

Use this same procedure for locating and carving the eyes of the bear. Draw on the right eye, carve it, and use the "paper trick", being careful to use the same centering points so your left bear eye is in proper alignment.

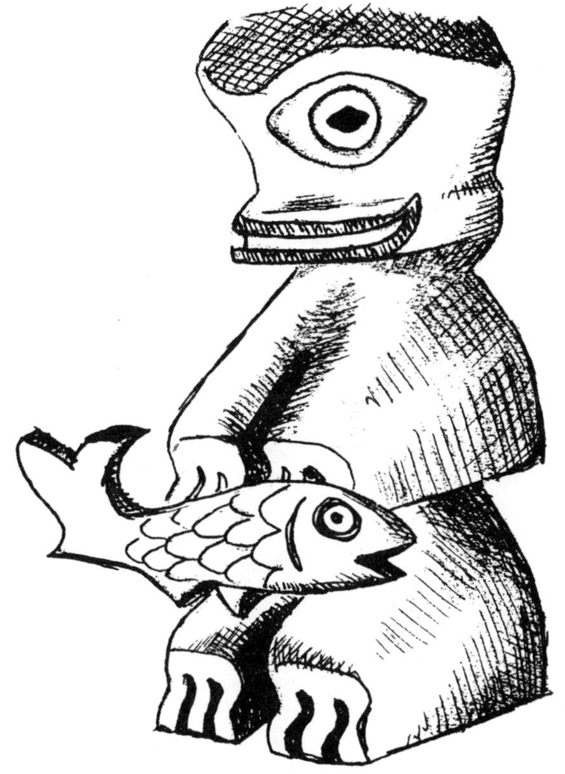

Bear.

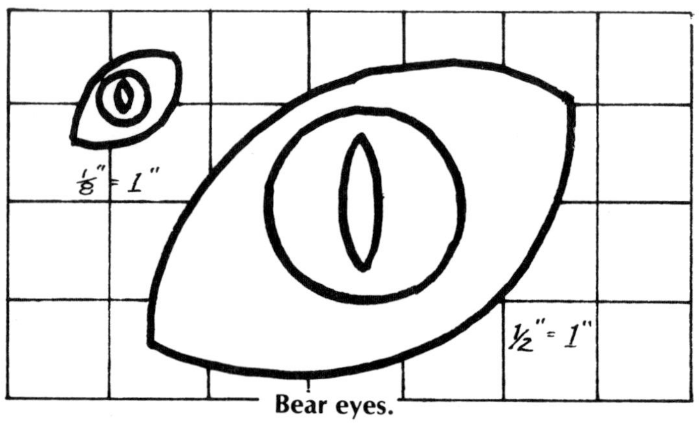

Bear eyes.

MOUTHS

The mouths of the thunderbird and bear can be done in the same fashion. Draw on your outline on one side. Carve it. Then use a sheet of paper to locate and carve the other side. I have not included templates for the mouths, as they will vary a lot from totem to totem, depending upon the shapes of beak and bear head you achieve. Simply look at the pictures shown; take your time.

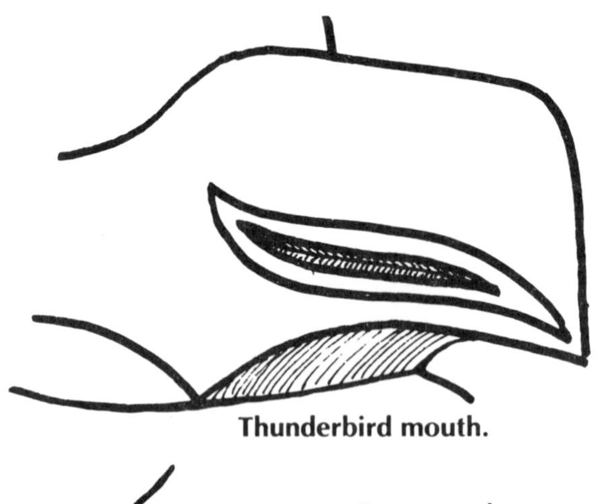

Thunderbird mouth.

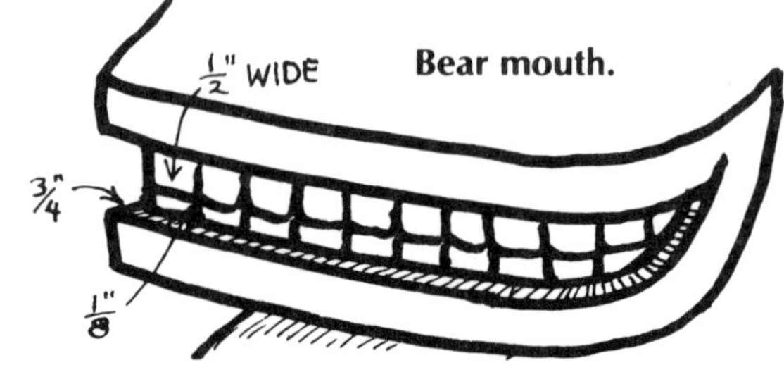

Bear mouth.

The teeth of the bear's mouth are outlined after you have the space between upper and lower lips carved out and smoothed about 3/4" deep. Teeth are about 1/2" wide and the upper teeth overlap the bottom ones 1/8" or so. Use a parting tool or carving knife to separate the teeth indentations of 1/8".

WINGS

You can take a trip to your friendly lumber yard and buy a fir or white pine board 2" by 8" by 10 feet. Cut off two feet of the board and save this for your salmon. Then cut the eight-foot remainder in two. These boards will then need to be properly joined and glued together so you have enough width for two wings 11" x 22". If you don't have a jointer, jig saw, drill, and clamps, you may want to get acquainted with a local woodshop teacher and see if you can use school equipment. The boards come from the lumberyard with slightly rounded edges. These need to be made flat so they can be tightly joined. A jointer serves this purpose. Ideally, dowels should be inserted as shown to give strength to the boards. A waterproof glue is used to glue the boards together and the boards are held tightly together by bar clamps for twenty-four hours. Unclamp and sand the boards smooth. On second thought, you may want to see if the teacher will assign these tedious tasks to a student as a project for credit or pay him something to prepare the wood for you.

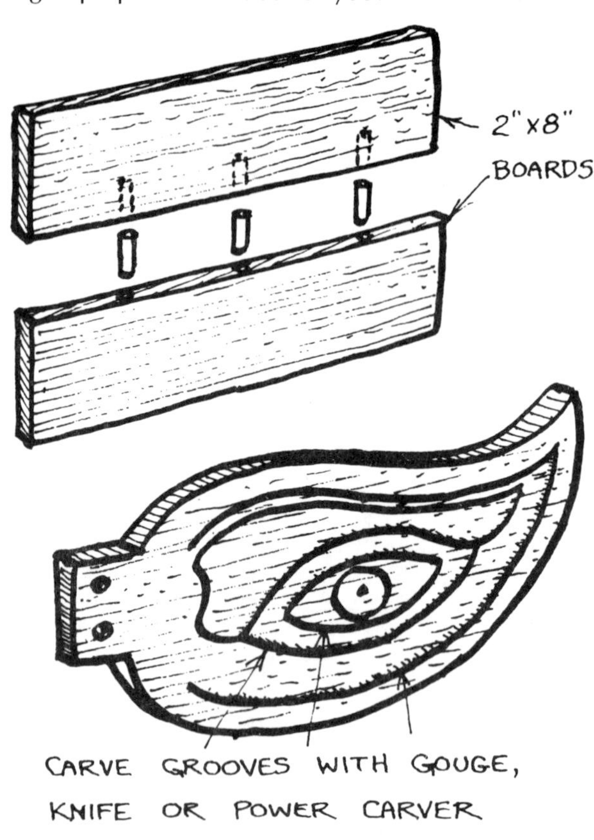

Carving the wings.

Using a method somewhat similar to that used for making the eyes, enlarge the template shown for the left wing. Use carbon paper under the template tacked to the board and draw the shapes in the wing on the board, using the best side of the board up. Then remove the template and draw over the lines of the template with a carbon underneath, but turned over, so the lines will appear on the other side of the template. Now, turn the template over and draw it (with carbon underneath) next to your left wing.

Use a jig saw to cut out the wing and a 1/4" gouge, knife, or flexible shaft electric tool to carve the grooves in the pattern. Sand and file the edges of the wing and interior grooves. The wings are attached after staining and painting are finished, using four 3/8" x 4" lag screws with washers.

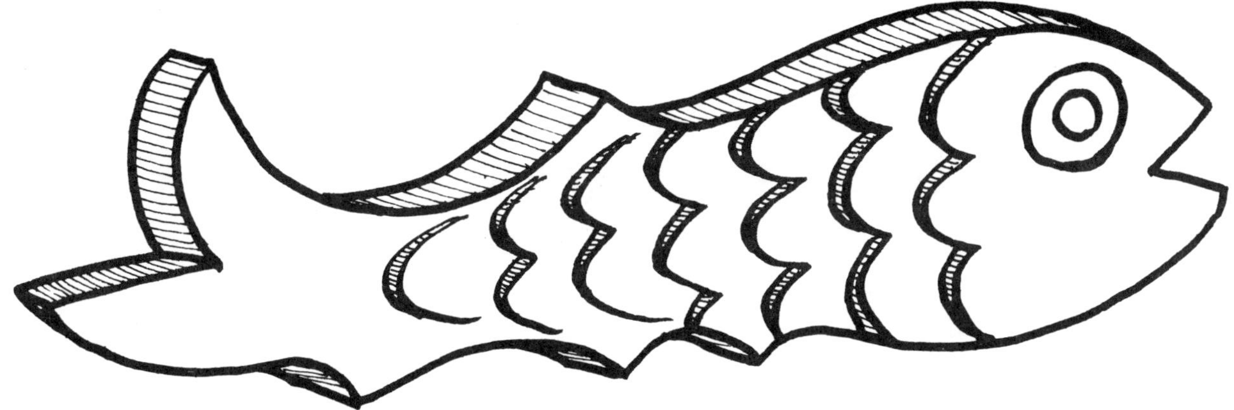

The salmon.

THE SALMON

The salmon is attached to the body of the bear by a 3/4″ dowel inserted just below the bear's upper paws. The salmon template needs to be drawn to scale and then traced over a carbon onto the piece of 2″ x 8″ you saved. The scales are carved very easily in the same manner as you did the feathers on the thunderbird belly. The eye consists of two circles, one for the outer eye outline and one for the pupil. Each circle is about 1/4″ in carved width or thickness around the edges. Sand the salmon and it is ready for finishing. Do not attach the salmon until the bear is stained and painted.

FINISHING

Look at the photograph in color on the cover. You can choose any colors, of course, but be careful not to use too many and try to follow through with some of the same colors in different phratries. Your color scheme will be very effective that way.

I start with a black walnut oil base stain over the entire log. Use two coats of oil base paints for the parts you choose to paint. Yellow is used for the thunderbird beak, part of the ears, the upper part of the wings, the top of the bear head, and bear feet. White is used for the thunderbird belly, the inner part of the eyes on both phratries, for the eyes in the wings, and the bear teeth. Gunmetal color is shown for the bear legs, for an outline in the wings, and for the pupils of the eyes. Green is used on the T-bird ears.

Two coats of marine varnish or other finish on the stained parts will add the final touches to your beautiful totem pole.

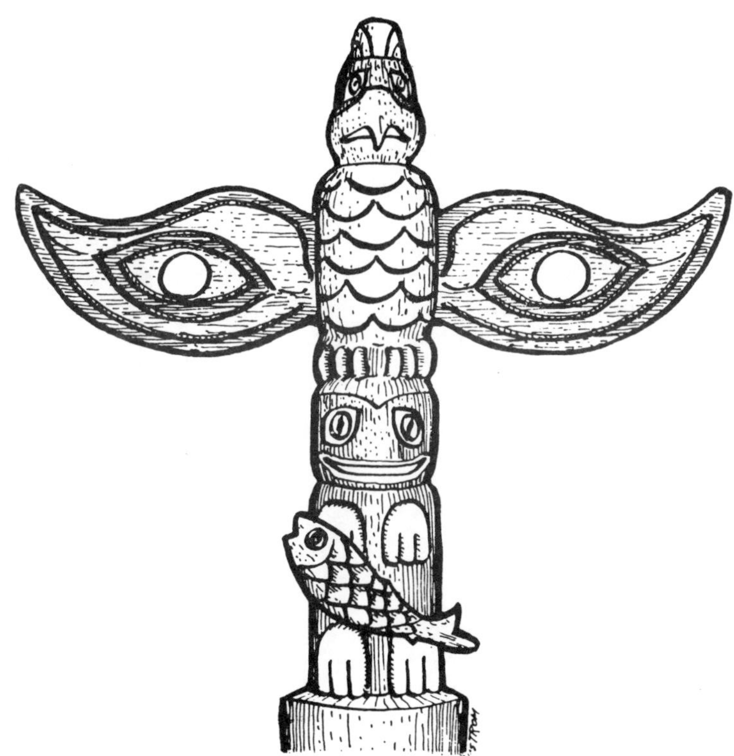

V
The Seven Foot
HAIDA ALASKAN TOTEM
"The Eagle Over Raven and Bear With Salmon"

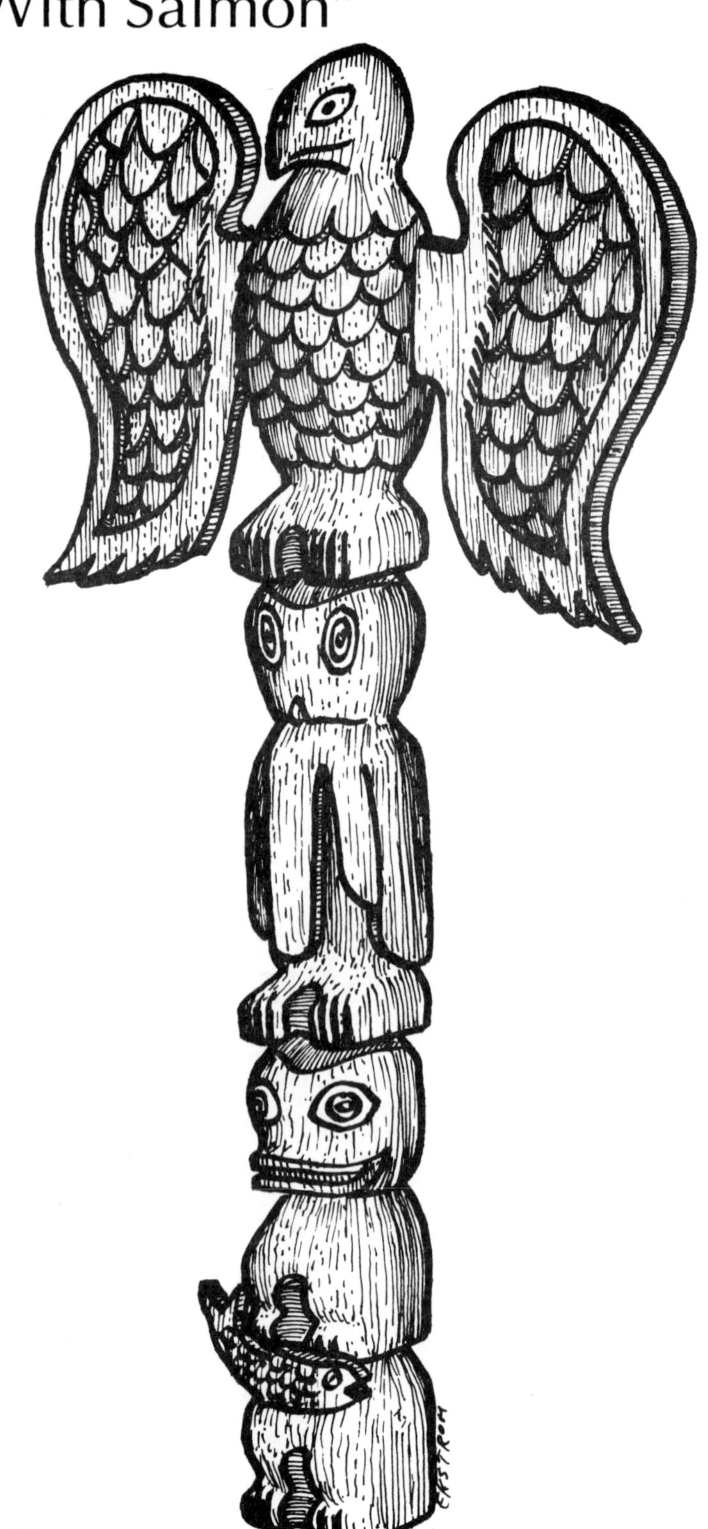

This totem is a little more complex to carve than the four foot one just described. However, you have already carved the bear-with-salmon, so you are experienced with his idiosyncracies. For this carving, we will assume some mastery of techniques of using the various tools and use a little less detailed description of the steps leading to its completion.

First, we need a timber approximately ten inches in diameter and seven feet long. Remember the suggestions for curing, taking off the bark, and sanding the log to achieve the fairly smooth and straight raw material for our carving.

The prepared log is laid across two sawhorses, stabilized, and the center line drawn the length of the log to center your phratries up-and-down the surface you choose to have facing its admirers.

SIDE VIEWS

Looking at the side-view pattern, lay out the basic pattern on both sides to show separation of phratries and depth of cuts as best you can. Note that, on this totem, you have to deal with the underside when rounding the eagle's head. You might use a soft pencil first to sketch on your pattern and then outline your final pattern with a magic marker for greater visibility. You have to develop an eye for proportion and depth when using a round log. I like to back off from the log, kneeling on either side, to see if my pattern looks right. Make any corrections and you are ready to carve.

THE EAGLE HEAD

The eagle head may be a challenge, so "what the heck," let's start there. Turn the log over with center line down and remove the wood above your pattern drawn on the back of the head, being careful to keep both sides symmetrical. You can use your chain saw, carefully, or fantail and other gouges. Give it a little "roundness" with your wood files before you turn the log back facing the sky. When you're satisfied, turn him back over.

LARGE CUTS

Now, let's remove the wood above the pattern drawn on the sides of the log using a similar procedure to that described for the four foot totem. Again, my preference is to use the chain saw to make cuts about 3/4" apart down close to the pattern, then horizontal cuts to remove this wood. Remember to go down the same dis-

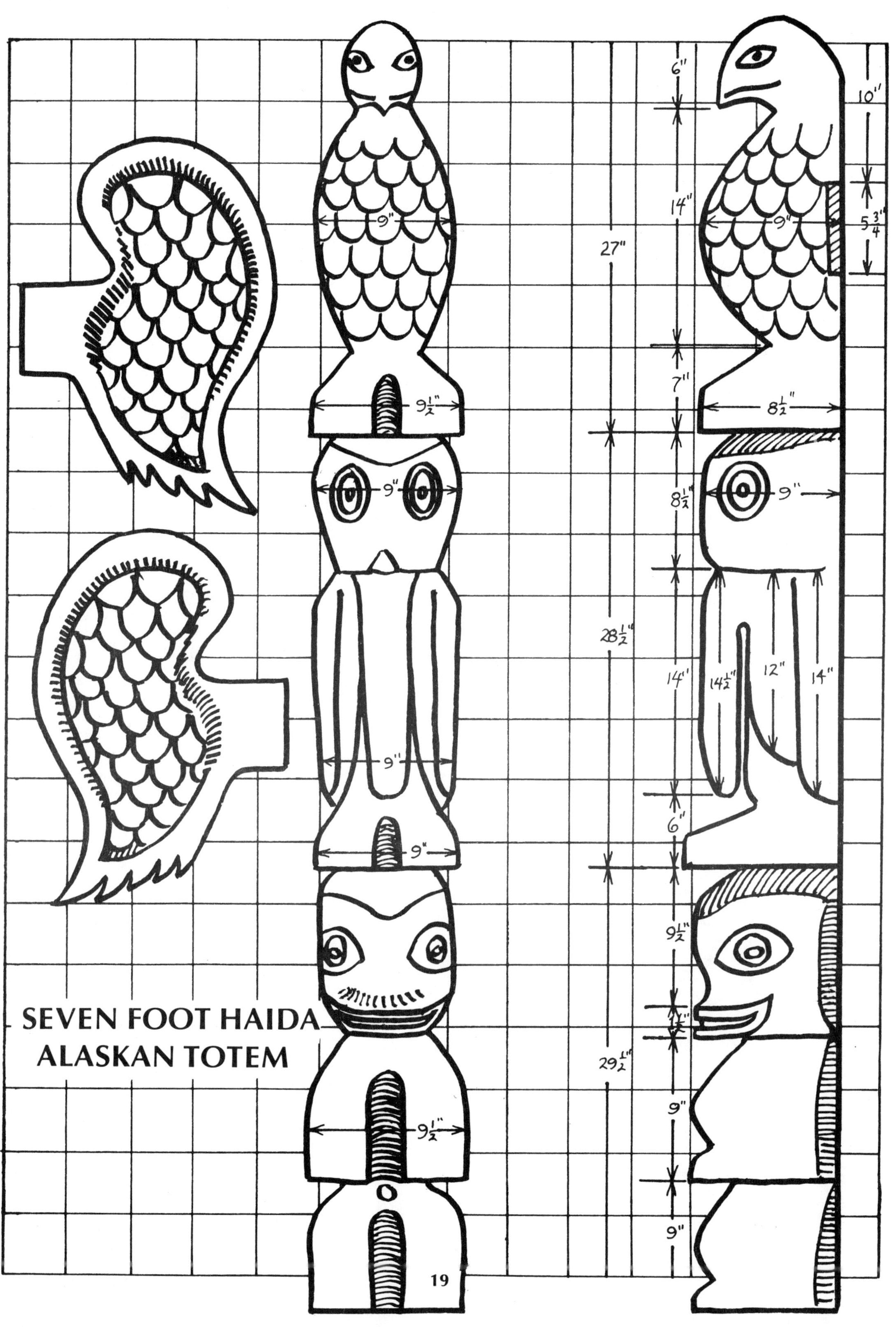
SEVEN FOOT HAIDA
ALASKAN TOTEM
6"
10"
14"
9"
5 3/4"
27"
7"
9 1/2"
8 1/2"
9"
8 1/2"
9"
28 1/2"
14"
14 1/2"
12"
14"
9"
6"
9"
9 1/2"
29 1/2"
9 1/2"
9"
9"

tance on both sides. Use of chisels and gouges, of course, provides a slower alternative to removing the waste material above your pattern. When you reach the pattern level, give this surface a rough sanding and re-draw your center line in preparation for further "labors of love". The side view surface is now achieved with a "square-off" surface something like that of the four footer.

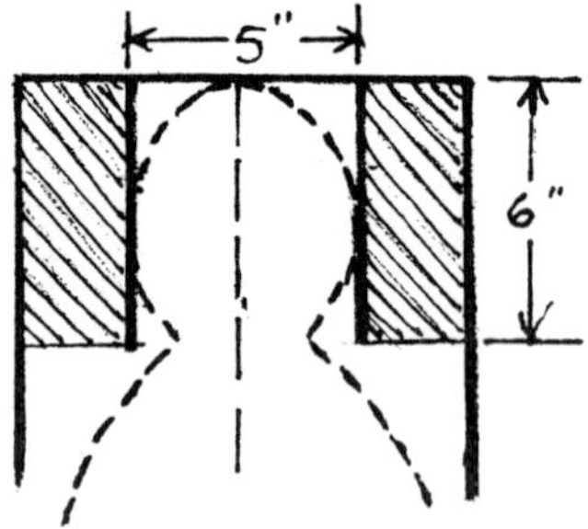

The eagle head.

Let's go back to the eagle head. The head is 5" wide at the widest point around the eyes. So, looking down on the bird, draw lines 2-1/2" from the center line and down 6" to block out the head. Standing at the sides, use the chain saw to make cuts in at the neck, being careful not to go too deep into the shoulder area. Then, at the head of the log, cut away the wood on both sides, leaving the blocked out 5" eagle head. Now, a few thoughts for your consideration.

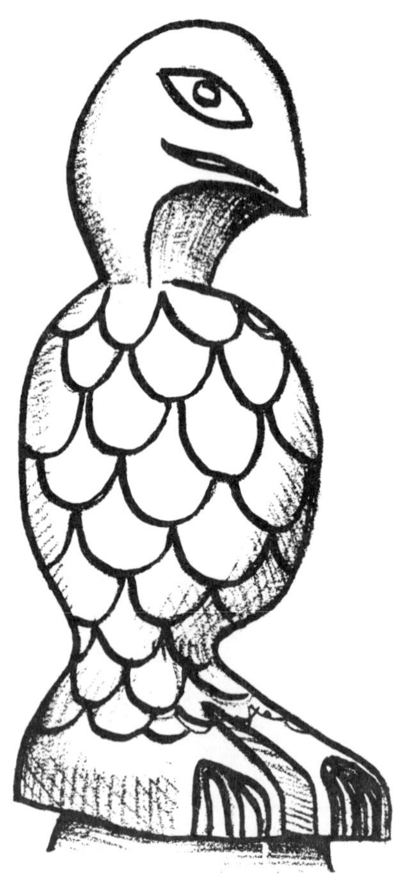

The eagle body.

SHAPING

There is no best way to describe how you go about shaping the eagle head, body, and feet—or how to round out the other phratries. Again, most carvers look at the drawings, patterns, and photographs frequently as they progress in their shaping and contouring work with chain saw, chisels, gouges, and knives. You have to find the methods you like best through trial and error.

Using a chain saw on the relatively fragile eagle head at this point could be "dangerous to his health." It might be best to use a 1/2" gouge, starting at the midpoint of the beak and whack away slowly, checking your progress with the pictures, and keeping the carving symmetrical.

The same is true for the underside of the beak, the neck, and the body of the eagle. Take your time. Round out the parts to make your bird look like the drawing. Be extra careful shaping the undersides of the beak that you keep them equidistant from the center line. Finally, separate the feet by cutting in to the depth of the raven's head (about 3") below. When you have this phratry done to your satisfaction, sand him down in preparation for later drawing on of eyes, mouth, feathers, and feet.

THE RAVEN

Okay, the raven is next. This one is a bit of a challenge, too. I like to start by laying out the contours on the top of the head and beak, then work down to the feathers on the sides. Let me explain.

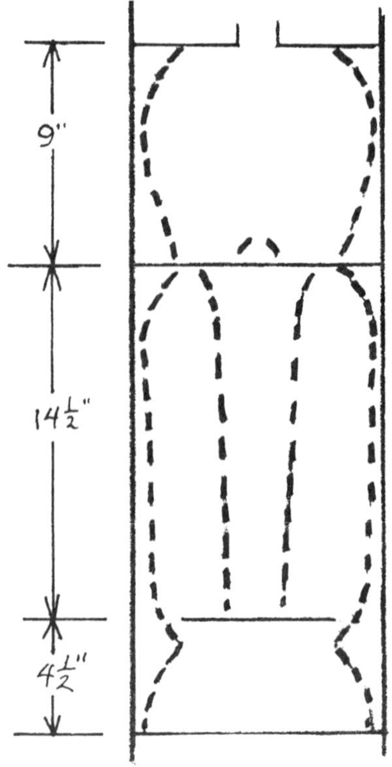

Measuring the raven.

Starting at the bottoms of the eagle toes, and using the center line for the raven, make markings down 9″ for the head, another 14-1/2″ for the beak, and finally 4-1/2″ more to mark the end of the feet.

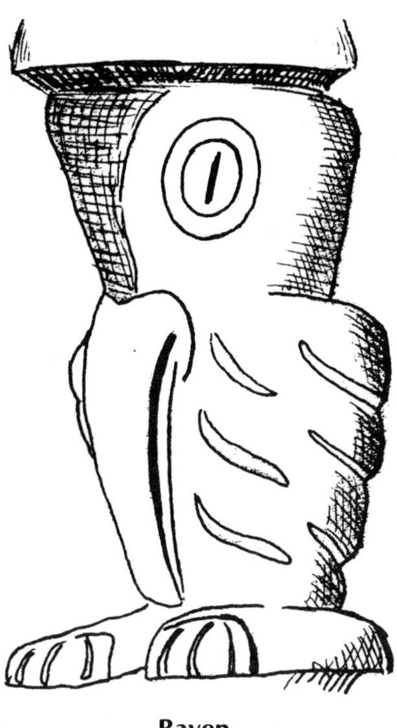

Raven.

Begin by cutting straight in about 1-1/2″ at the base of the eagle feet (front and sides) with a saw and making slanting cuts up to the depth of the cut at this level along with what will be the raven head from about 1-1/2″ down. Look at the drawing and you'll get the idea of how the raven's head slopes inward at the top on front and sides.

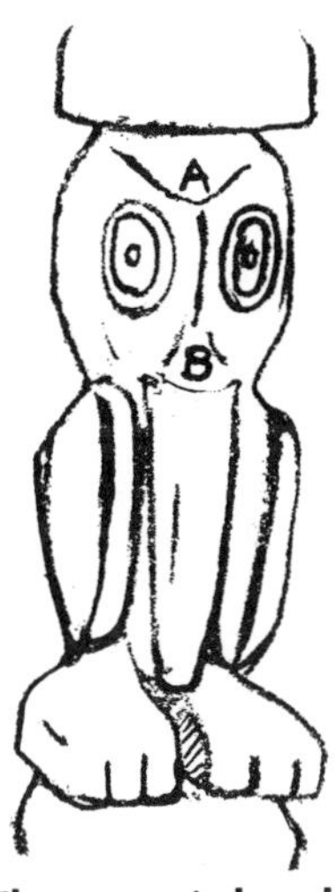

The raven's head.

Then, note how the head of the raven is shaped from the center line A-B. The face slopes away to either side from the rounded center-front. There are triangular shapes above at A and at B. Area A shapes the forehead of the raven and area B slopes in about an inch. The head can be shaped using gouges and rotary sanders.

BEAK

Now, lay out the beak. It should be 14-1/2″ long, about 3″ wide at the widest part of the top and 2″ at the base. The finished beak should slope in about an inch at the lower end. Carve away with a gouge (1/2″ is nice) on both sides of the beak to the same depth (about 3″).

On either side of the beak, use a gouge to round out the space where the feathers will be shown.

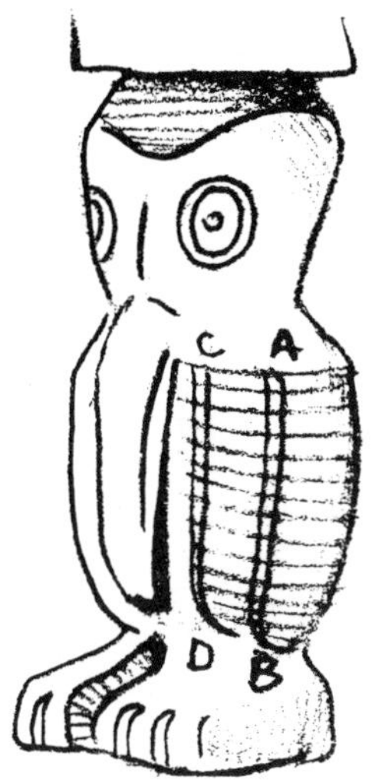

Carving the raven's wings.

WINGS

Now, doing the wings is tricky. Note that there are two wing levels on either side. The back wing curves down to about 14″ in length and the wing closest to the beak is about 12″ as it blends into the longer wing at the base. The back and middle parts of the wings should be about the same width. This means that if you went into the 10″ log about 3″ for the beak, you have about seven inches left. On a round log distances have to be estimated with the roundness as a consideration. Anyway, this seven inches or so gives us two wings about 3-1/2″ at the upper and middle areas on either side. The wings slope to the back near the bottom. Make lines A–B and C–D on one side of the beak. Using a gouge, cut down into the wood about 3/4″ along line A–B on the front or top side. Carefully bend the now indented surface at A B back outward toward the line C D as you shape the smaller wing. Then separate the smaller wing at C D from the area adjacent to the beak by cutting in about 3/4″ along C D around the beak. I hope I haven't confused you, but there doesn't appear to be a better way to explain this. Look at the drawings and do your best. After finishing one side, you may either make a pattern to do the other or measure carefully to maintain symmetry.

FEET

Separate the feet by cutting in about an inch in either side of the center line and being careful not to cut into the space below where the bear's head will be. Again, note the slope of the feet at front and sides. Wow, this one was different, wasn't it? Use wood files and sander to smooth the surfaces. Eyes and toes can be done later.

THE BEAR

The bear is next. If you carved the four-footer, you gained experience with our bear and salmon. Note that the dimensions are a little different for this bear. The head is 11 inches long and the distance from neck to upper paws is nine inches. Upper paws to the bottom is also nine inches. The carving procedure described last chapter for the bear can be used for this fellow, too.

Now, sand and smooth the whole thing in preparation for the features. The designs or patterns for eyes, mouth, wings, and salmon are shown in Chapter IV.

FEATURES AND FEATHERS

Note the placement of the eyes and mouth on the eagle. The eye is carved, using a Dremel or Foredom power tool with a #134 bit making a groove about 3/8″ deep, which outlines its shape and also that of the eyeball. You can use a knife or 1/4″ gouge. The mouth is carved with about the same width and depth of cut. Do one side, carve it, and use the paper-and-pencil rubbing technique to transfer the pattern to the other side using the beak center as a guide for symmetry.

The feathers on the eagle body and wings are achieved in the same manner as that described for the thunderbird belly. The feet of the eagle are pictured. Draw on your pattern and make 3/8″ grooves to outline the toes.

The eyes of the raven are round circles. Note the placement, make your drawing, carve one side, use the paper trick to make a pattern, and then do the other eye.

The toes of the raven are easy to do. Make three toes by making two grooves equidistant apart and cutting in while rounding the toes to your satisfaction.

Placement of the bear's eyes and feet were described in the last chapter. The drawing of one eye, carving, and aligning the other are techniques for which you are now a master. Right? So do these with confidence.

The salmon pattern shown in the last chapter can be used for this totem, also. The feathers are sculpted in the same manner and the eye is made of two circles, one for outer dimension and the other for the pupil. Each circle is about 1/4″ thick in outline. The salmon is attached after all parts are finished and stained or painted. A 3/4″ dowel joins the salmon to the bear, just below the upper feet.

THE WINGS

The wing pattern is shown. The wings are 15″ by 24″. You can purchase a 2″ by 8″ by 10′ pine or fir board from your local lumberyard for the wings and salmon. Have them cut it into two four foot lengths

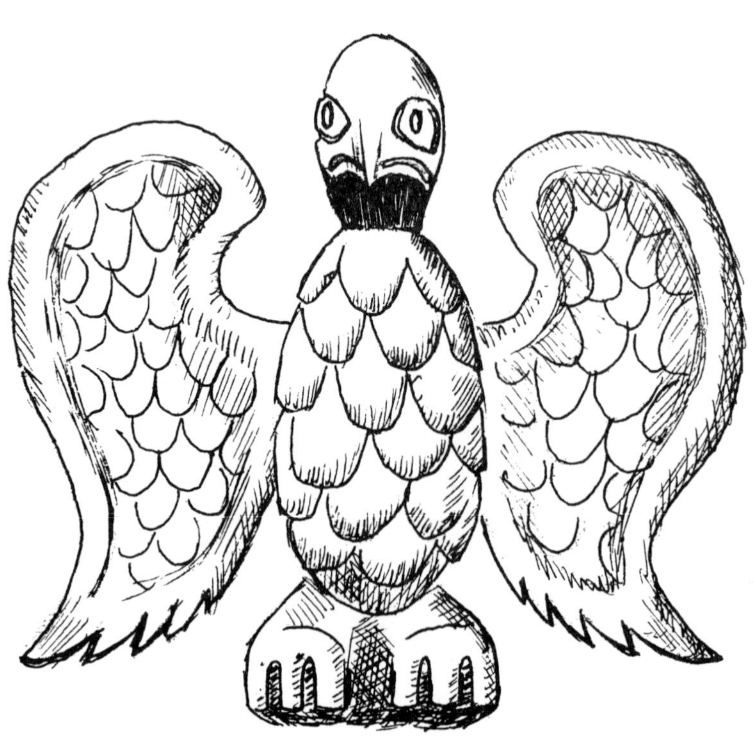

Haida eagle.

and a two foot length. Using the two four foot boards, with the edges planed for joining, dowels inserted for strength, glue them together with waterproof glue. You now have a board for the wings approximately 15″ by 48″. Make a pattern from the wing and draw it on the smooth side of the board, revising the pattern for right and left wings.

Notice how the wing is concave where the feathers will be. This area needs to be hollowed out to within about 1-1/2′ of the edges, using gouges and rotary sander before you draw on the feathers. When the wing is smoothly indented, draw on the feathers as shown and carve them as I have described several times before. Voila! You have your totem parts ready for staining, painting, and assembly.

FINISHING

Now for the finish. If your wood grain is very attractive, you may wish to stain the entire totem in walnut or another color and wax or varnish it without color. I prefer the combination of stain and oil base colors shown in the photograph on the cover. Stained areas, including the wings and salmon, are covered with two coats of marine varnish and painted areas get two coats of paint.

You may wish to make a base for the totem for greater stability. A piece of plywood 14″ x 14″ screwed to the bottom or a box-like base about 4″ by 14″ by 14 ″ would be nice. Assemble the wings with lag screws and washers. Glue on the salmon and you have a "best seller"

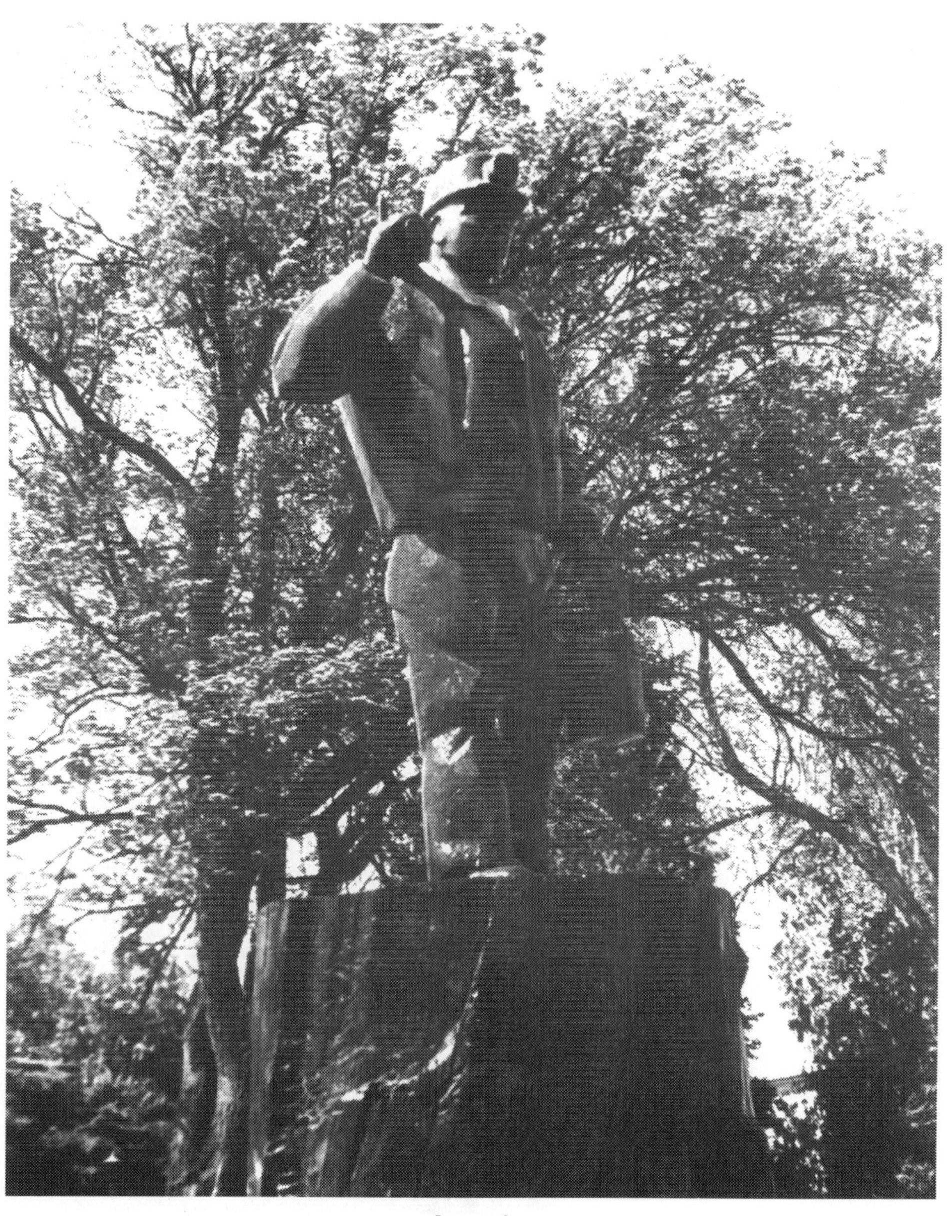

The Miner

Pg. 23

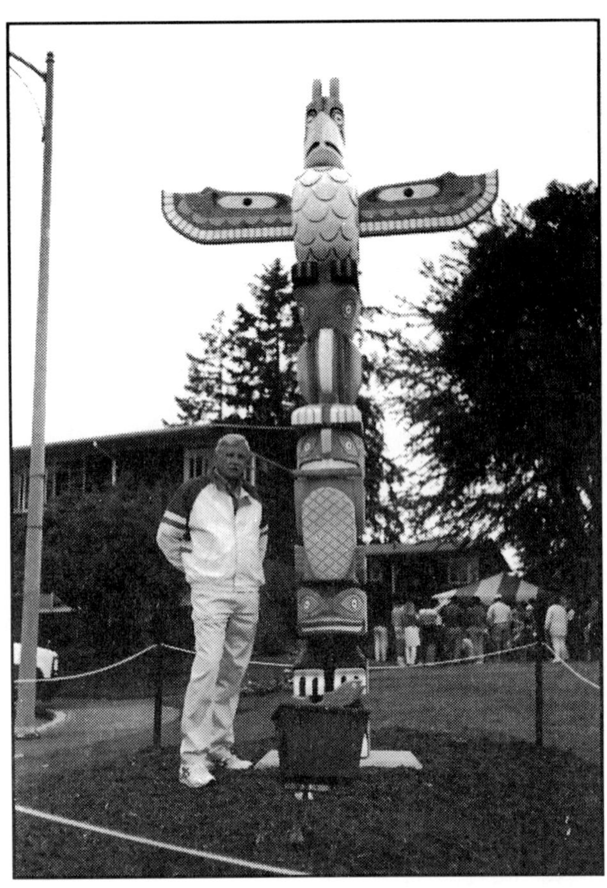

14 foot Mercer Island
totem installed.
Sculptor Walt Way at left.

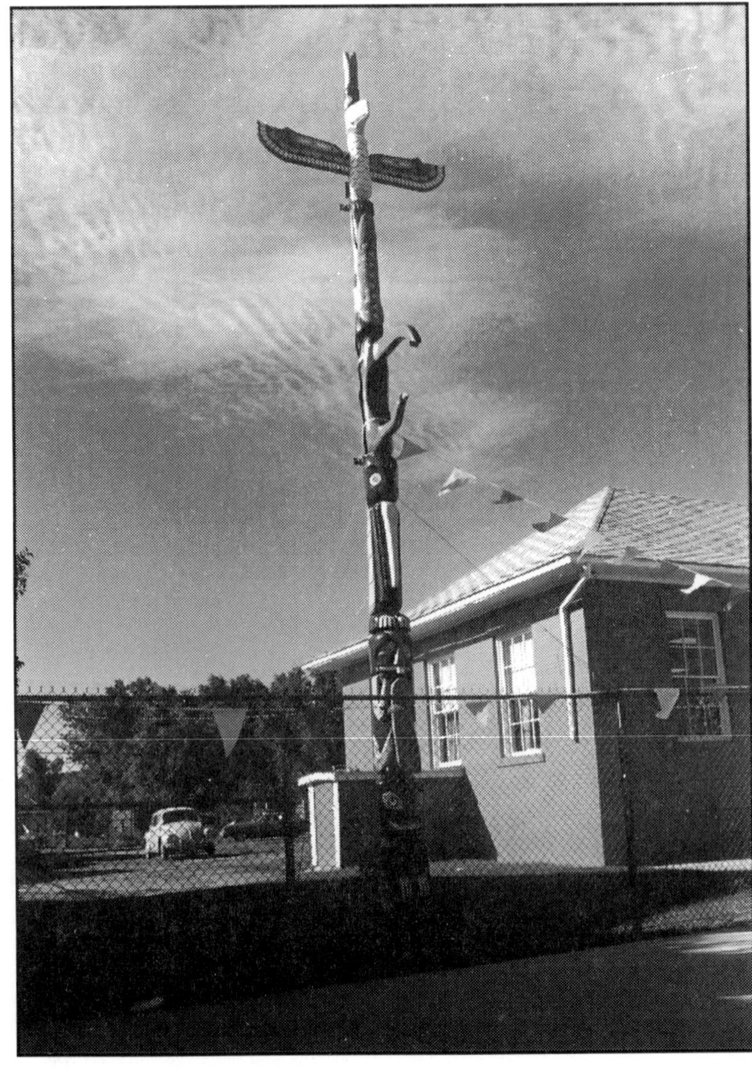

A 30 foot totem
carved by Walt Way.
Installed in front of school administration
building in Walsenberg, Colorado.

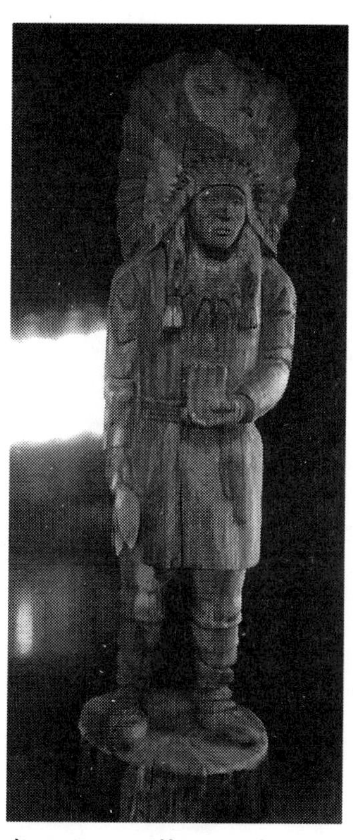

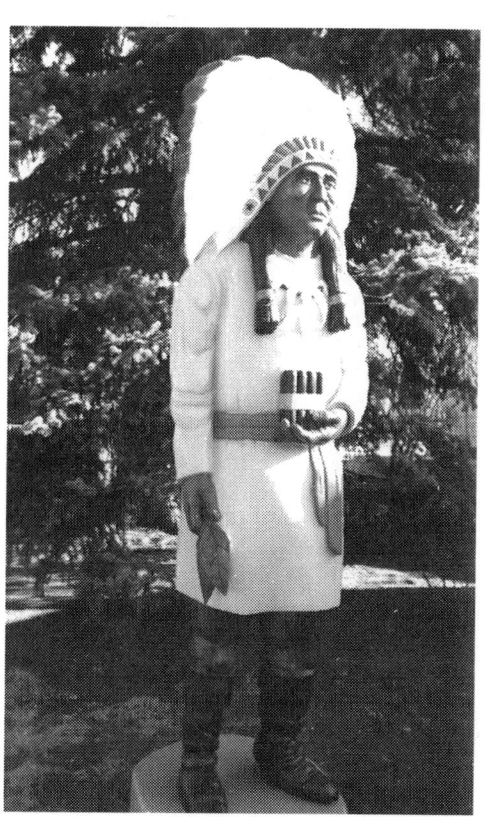

The Cigar Store Indian is an all-time favorite subject. As you become more proficient at carving, you may well wish to attempt one as a project.

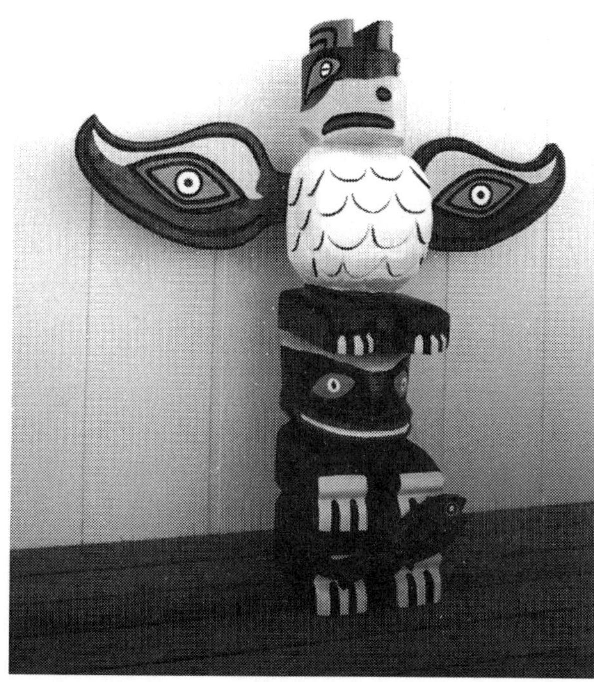

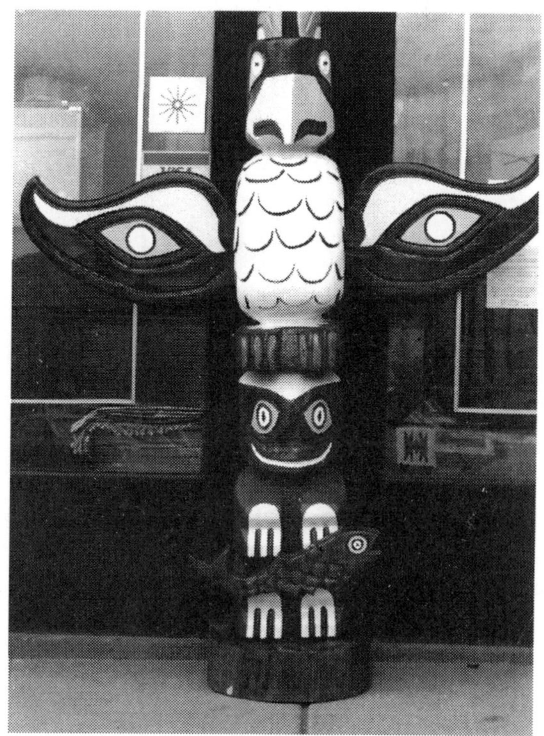

FOURTEEN FOOT HAIDA TOTEM

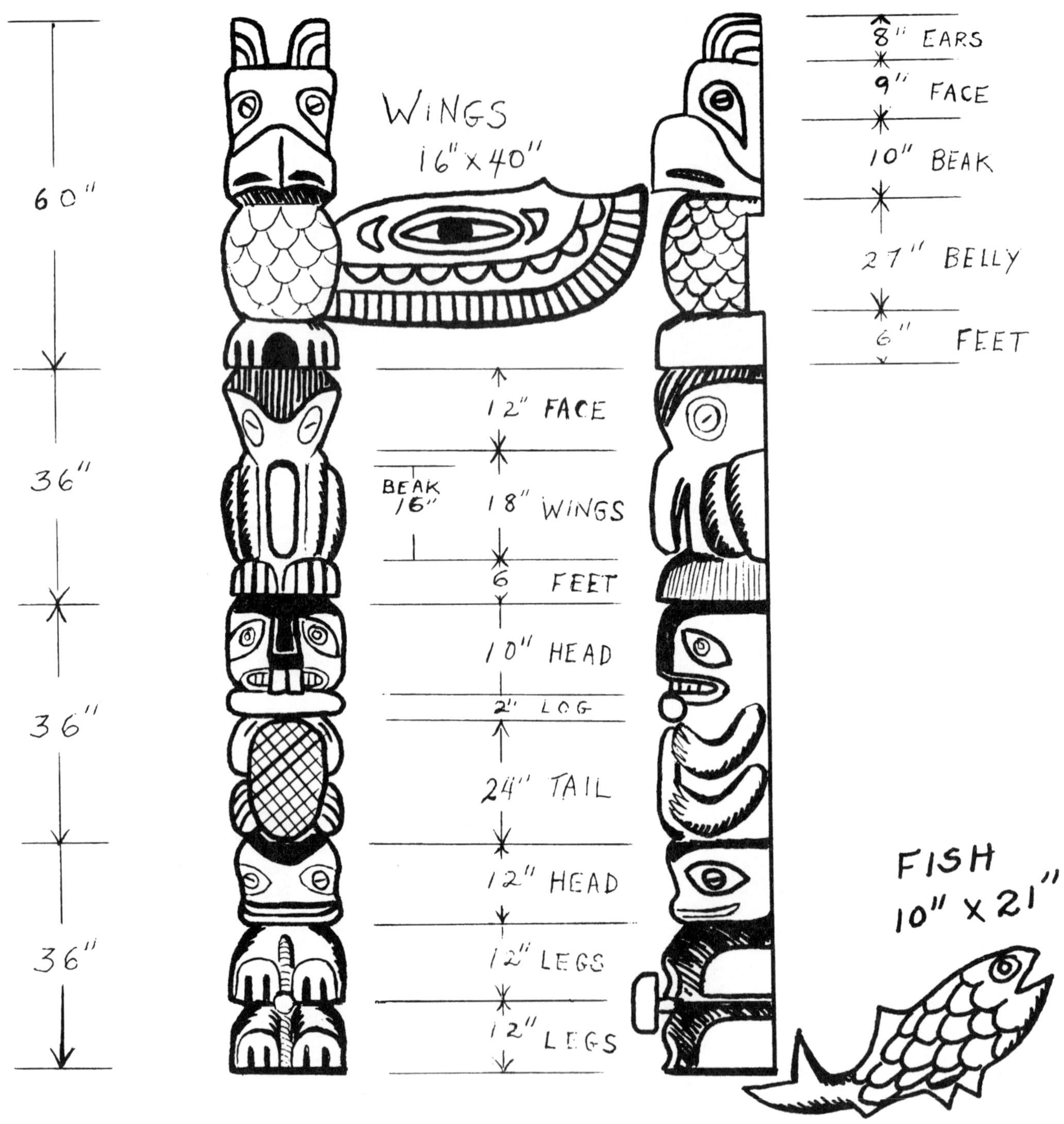

"This totem pole was carved by the author in the summer 1993 as an artist-in-residence project for Shorewood Apartments in Mercer Island, Washington. The phratries (top to bottom) are thunderbird, raven, beaver, and bear. A native red cedar log (16" x 16" x 14") was used. Red cedar was the log of choice for the early northwest Indians. Some of their totems would stand well over 100 feet in height.

VI
ADDENDA

FUTURE CARVINGS

What next? Before writing this book we had thought of including narrative and pictures of more totems and statues "in the round." Space became a problem and also the notion that maybe this is a topic for another book. We'll see.

My early totems were original designs and they showed it. You'll find it hard to beat the Northwest Indian phratries for beauty, simplicity, and meaning.

A suggestion. As you gain experience and confidence in your work, use the pictures in the books suggested in the bibliography or visit museums housing totem and make your own patterns for future carvings. With photographs of totems, you can scale them and their parts to the actual size you want.

Use various combinations of phratries up and down the length of the pole. Vary the size of the phratries depending upon the number you use and the length of the log. My thirty-footer has some of the same phratries we carved, together, in these pages and it has six phratries of about five feet each.

Well, this book has been both a difficult task to write and yet a labor of love, fellow carvers. Please, write or call me if you have questions, constructive criticisms, or just ideas to share. 'Til then, "happy carving".

WHERE TO BUY CARVING TOOLS

We could classify the sources for purchasing tools for carving into two broad categories: (1) Those you can most easily buy through catalog sales at stores like Sears or Montgomery Wards or by shopping in these and local hardware stores, and (2) tools rarely stocked in these stores, but which can be purchased through special catalogs. The catalogs are available at a small cost and several companies are listed below.

In the first category are the electric grinders, rotary sanders and sandpaper, drills and bits, chain saws and lubricants, and other common hardware items. I find Craftsman power tools at Sears hard to beat for quality and price. Both Sears and Wards have frequent sales when these tools can be purchased at good savings to the carver.

In the second category are the more esoteric carving tools such as chisels, gouges, mallets, carving knives, rifflers, miniature power tools, and the like. Again, one seldom find these tools at the local retail store or in general catalog sales. Here are some sources:

The Foredom Electric Company, Bethel, CT 06801
Dremel, Division of Emerson Electric Company, 4915 21st Street, Racine, WI 53406
Woodcraft, 313 Montvale Ave., Woburn, MA 01888
The Woodworkers' Store, 21801 Industrial Blvd., Rogers, MN 55374
The Woodcraft Shop, 2724 State St., Bettendorf, IA 52722
WOODCRAFT Catalog, Box 1686, Parkersburg, WV 26102-1686
Wood Carvers Supply Co., Box 7500, Englewood, FL 34295

BOOKS ABOUT TOTEMS

Reading about totems, the early native carvers, and the uses and meanings of this art form helps the carver to get a feeling for the work before you start.

Some of the available books are very inexpensive and yet provide a lot of information about this art of the Northwest Indians. Your public libraries may have additional books on the subject. Here are a few suggestions:

Barbeau, Marius Art of the Totem Pole Hancock House.

Barbeau, Marius The Modern Growth of the Totem Pole on the Northwest Coast, The Shorey Book Store, 110 Union Street, Seattle WA 98101.

Brindze, Ruth Story of the Totem Pole, Vanguard Press.

Crane, W. Totem Tales 1952, Shorey Book Store (see above).

Garfield, Viola E. and Forrest, Lynn Wolf and the Raven: Totem Poles of Southeastern Alaska University of Washington Press, Seattle, WA.

Lloyd, J.P. Message of an Indian Relic: Seattle's Own Totem Pole, Shorey Book Store (see above).

Mac Dowell, Lloyd W. Alaskan Totem Poles, The Shorey Book Store (see above).

Macnair P., Hoover A., Neary K. The Legacy: Tradition and Innovation in Northwest Coast Indian Art Published in cooperation with the Royal British Columbia Museum Douglas & McIntyre Vancouver/Toronto University of Washington Press Seattle.

INDEX

About the Author

Walt Way, a retired educator, has as his first priority house-husbanding for his wife, Judy, a teacher of Spanish. He works in his studio located in their home in Elizabeth, Colorado at his avocation of sculpting totem poles, life-size statues, and Indian busts, while also working on a second book which "branches out" (he likes puns) from this book to describe many unique projects he has done and to tell the stories behind their creation.

Walt enjoys sharing ideas about the art of wood-carving with others. He says a favorite commission was that of the artist-in-residence project at Mercer Island, Washington, where he had daily visits with residents and other people from as far away as Scotland while carving the 14-foot totem pictured here in a record twenty-one days.

Readers who may want to discuss ideas about carving or to commission a project are invited to contact him by mail at Post Office Box 1079, Elizabeth, Colorado, or call at (303) 646-3542.

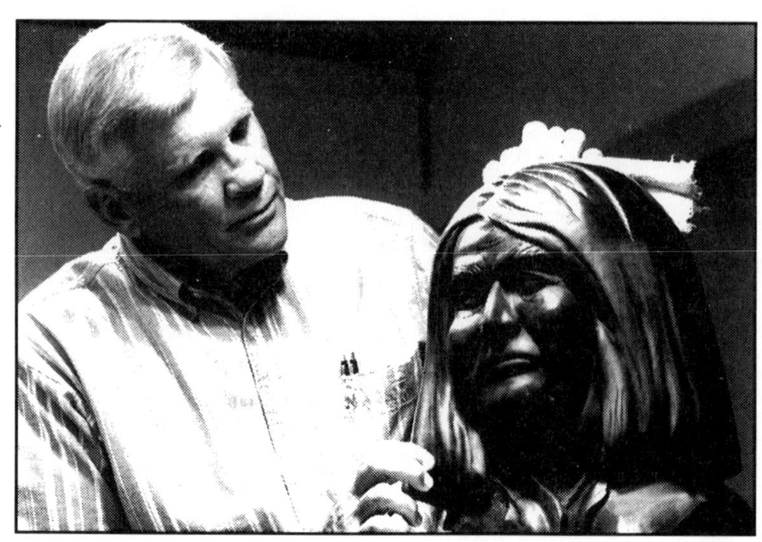

The author with a bust of an Indian carved from Walnut (photo by Kathy Heister)